LOVE
HAS COME AGAIN

MARSHALL, MORGAN & SCOTT

TO DEB

and

TO MY FAMILY

whether by birth or marriage or because
the Holy Spirit has especially given us
to one another, it makes no difference

I LOVE YOU

LAKELAND
Marshall, Morgan & Scott
a member of the Pentos group
1 Bath Street, London EC1V 9LB

Copyright © Jim Bigelow 1978
First Published 1978

ISBN 0 551 00792 3

Biblical quotations, unless otherwise stated, are from the Revised Standard
Version of the Bible, copyrighted 1946, 1952, © 1971, 1973 by the National
Council of the Churches of Christ in the USA and used by permission.

Quotations from the following are used by permission:
'If' by Rudyard Kipling from *The Definitive Edition of Rudyard Kipling's
Verse* by permission of The National Trust and the Macmillan Co. of
London and Basingstoke; 'Eleanor Rigby', words and music by John
Lennon and Paul McCartney, © 1966 Northern Songs Ltd. for the World;
'You Followers of the Bearded Christ' by John Witmer from *Rappings* (ed.
Robert Webber) © Tyndale House Publishers, Wheaton, Illinois; 'Taking
Without Giving', 'Loneliness' and 'My True Feelings' by Graham Kendrick
© Graham Kendrick 1976 and featured on his LP album *Breaking of the
Dawn*, Dove 36. Further details are available from Dovetail Records, 33
West Hill, Wandsworth, London, SW18 1RB; 'Will You Be My Friend?'
and 'I Knew This Kid' from *Will You Be My Friend?* by James Kavanaugh,
copyright © 1971 by James Kavanaugh. Reprinted by permission of the
publisher, E. P. Dutton; *The Little Prince* by Antoine de Saint Exupéry,
trans. by Katherine Woods and published by William Heinemann Ltd.
Every attempt has been made to obtain permission for the following:
'As Others See Us' by Basil Dowling from *Voices: The Third Book* (ed.
Geoffrey Summerfield); 'Bridge Over Troubled Waters' by Paul Simons
(Charing Cross Music Inc.).

Made and printed in Great Britain by
Cox & Wyman Ltd, London, Reading and Fakenham
8710R51

Contents

Preface

It was my intention to thank everyone who had made a significant contribution to the book. But, when I began to try to identify each one and the particular contribution they had made, I despaired! There have been so many who have shared in the living lessons from which the book has been written. My constant partner who has shared every lesson with me is my wife Deb. We've learnt together to open our hearts and life and home. Her wholehearted support of all that I have ever undertaken has meant that I have never had to turn aside from anything the Lord's given me to do. There are no words to express fully my love and gratitude to her.

I'm grateful, too, to all of those with whom we shared life at Post Green. Their love and care opened Deb and me to so much that the Lord wanted to teach us and sustained us through some of the more painful lessons.

I am especially grateful to Andy and Jill Newman and to Paul and Lita Ogle who have shared their love and their lives so fully with Deb and me. It is their love which has made me know that the ideals and dreams presented throughout the book are, in fact, available to those who are prepared to open their hearts and lives to one another.

I would also like to express my love and gratitude to our family and friends, especially our children, on the West Coast of the USA. We have now lived away from them for several years. I pray that the book will in some way compensate them for the years of separation. I am, certainly, aware of the contribution they have made to my life and ministry and, thus, to the book.

I would, like to thank Deb and Lita for the hours they have spent reading and typing the manuscripts and Paul for his many comments and suggestions at every stage of writing and revision. Finally, I would like to thank Malcolm and Trisha Dale and Andy and Jill for proof reading the final manuscript. Without the love and encouragement of each one of these, I could never have persevered to finish the task.

Foreword

It is the Spirit that gives life – He is the Life-giver; the flesh conveys no benefit whatever – there is no profit in it. The words (truths) that I have been speaking to you are spirit and life (John 6: 63, The Amplified Bible).

But the natural, nonspiritual man does not accept *or* welcome *or* admit into his heart the gifts *and* teachings *and* revelations of the Spirit of God, for they are folly (meaningless nonsense) to him; and he is incapable of knowing them – of progressively recognizing, understanding and becoming better acquainted with them – because they are spiritually discerned *and* estimated *and* appreciated (1 Cor. 2: 14, The Amplified Bible).

During the sixty years of my Christian life the truth of the above words has helped me repeatedly to recognise truth and error in the writings of men. Therefore, I am glad to have the privilege to write this foreword to the record of the experiences and discoveries of Jim and Deb. I have seldom read a book or manuscript with which I agree so much that I almost wish I had written it myself. But I know that I could not have written so many glorious truths so beautifully in both scriptural and academic terminology and yet so simply that they can be understood by the unlearned as well as the learned.

From these pages I have learnt that the same truths are often revealed to servants of the Lord who have travelled along totally different paths through life. The leaves of this book remind me of the leaves of the 'tree that is planted by the pure river of water of life . . . which were for the healing of the nations' (Rev. 22: 1–2, AV). There is no attempt to cover up or justify human weakness and failure, yet the fallen and disappointed are led back to the paths of righteousness and to more abundant life. Here the reader will find the truth about the *renewal* of the individual, the community, the

Church, the nations, and the world that God so loved that he gave his only begotten Son.

For the last quarter of a century, I have constantly drawn wisdom from a lesson I learnt in a very personal and intimate conversation with the late Professor Karl Barth in Basel, Switzerland. He asked me to be open and frank with him in discussing the work of the Holy Spirit in our lives. He said, 'I am not a fundamentalist.' Then I asked him who he considered to be a real *fundamentalist.* He answered, 'He is a person who knows some scripture and thinks he has arrived and that there is no more to learn or to experience. If you disagree with him, he says you are lost; if you tell him you have experienced more than he confesses, he thinks you have gone astray.' Then I asked him whether there comes some point of 'arrival'. Quickly he responded, 'No, there is no point of arrival because Jesus Christ is the *way* and there is no terminal. You must continue to go along this way, and the further you go, the more liberating truth you discover. The more you become liberated by the truth, the more abundant life you enjoy.' That day in the study of the old professor, I gave up the idea of arrival and began to look ahead to learn more from the valleys and peaks of truth which liberate from the bondage of isolation and ignorance. Since then, I truly enjoy more abundant life in the Lord Jesus Christ by the Holy Spirit. I trust that all who read these pages will learn that there is really no terminal but that they must ever go forward in 'faith, hope, and love'.

I pray that those who are so engrossed with the Holy Spirit that they tend to disregard the fact that there is also a spirit in man, and for whom the study of psychology is meaningless and even dangerous, will be able to learn from these pages that there is a reconciliation between psychology and theology – between the spirit of man and the Spirit of God. Then I would appeal to the psychologists, who seek to deal only with human spirit and disregard the Holy Spirit, to become wise from the lessons learnt by my friend Jim, the psychologist who wrote this book.

David J. du Plessis

October 1977

1. Let Me be Honest

I was pastoring a small Pentecostal church in Southern California when Russia shot *Sputnik* into space. In a fashion which has become typical, America determined to catch up with, and for that matter surpass, Russia as soon as possible. The means by which this was to be done was, of course, education and technology. Suddenly, higher education was available on a broader scale than ever before in the nation's history. You could take advanced courses in anything from nuclear fission to basket weaving, and the government would pay for it, if only you would continue to study. Consequently, most of the young people in my congregation began attending either college or university, and I began to hear terms and concepts which were completely foreign to me. My own preparation for the ministry had been a three-year Bible College training programme, and it was evident that this new generation was going to be speaking and thinking in terms for which I was not prepared.

I knew nothing, at that time, about the charismatic renewal in the historic churches which was then just in its infancy. As far as I knew, if the message of the 'Spirit-filled life' was going to be saved from oblivion in this new era of the academic degree, we Pentecostals were going to have to do it! So, after prayerful consideration, my wife Elizabeth and I agreed that I should enroll in an advanced course of study in order to acquaint myself with the world of higher education. I had no particular educational goals; I simply determined that I would continue to study as long as the Lord made it clear that that was what he wanted me to do.

I must be very honest and say that, by the time I resumed my education, I already had begun to be somewhat disappointed in the Church as I knew it. I knew that we were speaking very little, if at all, to the real hurt and pain of human existence. Actually, I was just in my mid-twenties at the time, and I'm not at all sure I really knew what the heart cry of loneliness and fear was all about – much less how to speak to it. But I did know that the stock answers – *more*

9

prayer, *more* Bible reading, and *more* involvement in the church programme – left many people dissatisfied and still searching; and I wasn't sure whether the fault lay in the way *I* presented the 'answers' or in the way *they* failed in carrying them out. But it simply wasn't working, and I knew it.

Up to that time, the extent of my knowledge about the field of psychology consisted of what I read in the *Reader's Digest*. I knew that psychology was credited with an ability to probe into deep human problems; and, since many pastors and church leaders were at that time using such terms as *Christian psychology* and *pastoral counselling*, I decided that psychology was the area with which I should acquaint myself. Needless to say, it was a real eye-opener to me as I became aware of the various fields of theoretical and research psychology, as well as that of clinical psychology and psychotherapy.[1] Nevertheless, it was the overall willingness amongst psychologists to acknowledge real human problems and to expose them to as realistic and objective a review as possible which captured my interest in the field.

In order to be near the college where I was to begin my studies, I transferred to the pulpit of a small church in a suburb of Los Angeles, California. Those were exciting and busy years. In addition to my pastoral duties, I took classes five days a week and tried to give as much time as possible to my wife and our two children, David and Michele, who were both at school by that time. Those years were rewarding in many ways. I had not been particularly clever at studies during my earlier school education, and so it was a very real surprise to discover that advanced studies were both a challenge and a real joy. I saw this return to studies as fitting into an overall pattern of God's will for my life, and I'm sure that that factor made a major contribution to the academic success of those first years. As a scholastic award, I was offered, at the conclusion of my second year, a full tuition scholarship to Whittier College, also near Los Angeles. That was the beginning of an association which was to continue for as long as I remained in the academic field. During those same two years, the church I was pastoring grew and prospered, all the more thrilling because I was so personally involved in my studies. Nevertheless, a larger Sunday School, a growing congregation, and suggestions to build larger church facilities could not offset the growing conviction that the real issues of human suffering and the longing for something more out of life were not being met by the 'church programme'.

The church continued to grow until it was evident that further growth would require new church buildings. A congregation which needs to build new facilities and a pastor who is carrying a full academic schedule of study can be a difficult combination. It was a hard decision to leave a congregation which had become so very dear; but, by that time, I knew what the Lord's priorities were for my life. Thus, in 1962, I assumed the pulpit of another church, also near Los Angeles, where it appeared that no building programme was imminent. Within two years, however, the congregation was talking of the need for new facilities – this time due to the age and condition of the main church building. I was in the midst of a Master's Degree at the time and so, again, transferred to a near-by pulpit in order to continue to follow the Lord where my education was concerned. I must add that there were always those, in each church where I pastored, who faithfully worked along with me in order to make it possible for me to give so much of my time and energy to further education. There were always men and women who seemed to feel that any contribution which they made to my education was somehow their way to speak to this generation. I shall never be able to repay or thank them enough for their love and help during those very busy years. To whatever purposes the Lord may use my education, I will always be aware that I didn't do it by myself and that I am never speaking for myself alone.

In 1966, two major events, along with my continuing concern for the effectiveness of the Church's message, culminated in my resignation from the pulpit altogether. A few weeks before I received my Master's Degree from Whittier College, Elizabeth died of cancer. We had prayed and fought her illness for four years prior to her death, and we had seen an outstanding miracle which our doctor acknowledged. Then, rather quickly, the Lord took her. Before her death, however, Elizabeth and I had talked and prayed about what step I should take next in my education, if the Lord were to open a further door to me. Therefore, when I was offered a full-subsistence study grant on the day following her funeral, I knew the decision I was to make. The grant required full-time study, and so I resigned my pulpit, and the children and I moved nearer my family and

11

the university at which I was to pursue a doctorate in psychology.

The following years were both sad and happy, empty and full. I continued a working relationship with Whittier College while studying at Claremont Graduate School and University Center. Thus, by the time I completed my doctorate in December 1969, I was teaching full-time in the Psychology Department at Whittier; I had married Deb who, along with her parents and brothers and sisters, had attended the church where I had last pastored; and David was at High School and Michele at Junior High School. We bought a new home near the coast; and, in addition to my duties at the college, I became an associate pastor to a friend of mine in the town where we lived. Life, at that point, took on a feeling of stability and permanence.

The honeymoon with psychology was fairly brief. It is true that psychology has labels for many (perhaps most) human problems, and it is also true that psychology is not embarrassed to talk about them. The major flaw in psychology's attempts to deal with the individual and his problems and pain is a rather subtle one. Underlying most approaches to therapy is an assumption which holds that *insight* (in and of itself) into the dynamics of a problem is health, or at least the means to achieving health. That is to say, it is generally believed that, if a person understands when and why he started behaving in certain ways and what the troublesome behaviour continues to mean to him, he is well, or certainly on the road to health. This rather simplistic ideal can be very enticing; and, when you begin to see and hear people openly discussing their very personal problems with apparent ease and understanding, you really do believe you've found something! It's only after a while that you realise that, with all this 'insight' and a full set of appropriate labels, people continue to live with their problems. The labels may help them cope and help to reduce some of the mystery which so often induces fear, but the basic problems very often remain, albeit neatly named and pigeonholed.

It is a frustrating and disheartening state of affairs to stop and look back on three years of theological training, ten years of study in psychology (as well as a new teaching career), and thirteen years of pastoring (and be called both *Reverend* and *Doctor*) and feel as though you've missed finding consistent answers to man's basic loneliness and fears caused both by loving and not being loved. I think my view of life, at that time, was that sin had made such havoc of the human state that one simply endured; took the more materialistic blessings in life as God the Father's way of saying, 'I love you and I want to somehow off-set the pain'; and waited for heaven which, finally, would be better than this!

Then, in the summer of 1972, Deb and I were invited to travel to England, and I was asked to speak at two youth camps which were to be held at Post Green in Dorset. It was to be a sort of 'working holiday' after which I would return to Southern California and Whittier College, where I was to be the Director of the Student Advisement Center, and all would be 'business as usual'. What actually happened was that the Lord used that summer to introduce Deb and me to the renewal of his Church and to begin a very personal renewal in our own lives.

When we arrived at Post Green, we found a team of ministers from a variety of church backgrounds and an even larger number of laymen all working together for the renewal of the Church. Many things about Post Green were unorthodox by any historic standard. For one thing Post Green is not the name of a 'church' but rather a large country house which is the home of Sir Tom and Lady Faith Lees. The work there had started about six years before as a home Bible study which had grown beyond all expectations. Many of the smaller meetings at this time were held in the drawing room, while the larger meetings were held in a large canvas dome which had been erected at the side of the house. Another unusual fact was that the leadership was shared amongst a sort of 'inner team' rather than provided through any one leader, with most decisions being made in rather large team meetings. Furthermore, most of the inner team, and many of the larger group, lived within a mile or two of Post Green and one another so that there was a daily life amongst them rather than a 'Sunday-plus-mid-week-service' relationship. The desire for openness and honesty amongst them was something I had only glimpsed occasionally in sensitivity and encounter-group sessions.

The most unorthodox behaviour of all, however, was the open and simple exchange of affection within the whole fellowship. We seldom saw a handshake, but hugs – and even

13

kisses – abounded. Deb and I were introduced to this more forthright display of affection when we, along with the other staff members, moved into Post Green itself just before the start of the first camp. All of the other staff members had their children with them, and in the evening everyone would gather informally in the kitchen to have a hot drink and to say goodnight to one another, particularly to the older children who were sleeping outdoors in tents. Before going off to bed, the children would hug and kiss *everyone* goodnight. I must add that the 'children' ranged in age from a babe in arms to a young man about twenty-one years of age who was built like a Mac Truck. Up to that point, I had never been hugged and kissed goodnight by a twenty-one-year-old 'Mac Truck' – especially one which didn't belong to me! However, several rather simple mental adjustments helped me cope with the situation. One was to say to myself, 'Oh well, when in Rome . . .', another was to remind myself that I would only be at Post Green for two weeks, and yet another was to reassure myself that after all these 'goodnights' only happened once a day! The one thing I wasn't at all sure of, however, was whether this goodnight ritual was something unique to Post Green or if it was typical for British children in general (I have since sorted that one out!).

The next instance in which I became aware of the more relaxed expressions of affection was when the camp actually began, and I observed the staff (speakers, counsellors, and maintenance crew alike) as they talked and prayed with the young people who had come to the camp. Many of these young people had come because they needed someone to talk to, while others had come just for a good time but found that in this atmosphere of love and concern they, too, wanted someone to talk and pray with. The thing which made watching these encounters unusual was seeing staff members with their arms around a young person weeping or laughing with them without any apparent embarrassment at all. All of my years of training told me that this was entirely wrong. In my theological preparation I had been taught that 'sheep and shepherd do not mix' and that 'familiarity breeds contempt', and in my psychological training I had been taught that a good counsellor remains objective and does not get emotionally involved with his client. It was evident that either no one had taught this staff the 'proper' way to give counsel or that they were deliberately flaunting the rules! At any rate, all of this really didn't concern me, since I would only be around for the two weeks of camps. All I had to do was somehow to blend in with the scenery and not be too conspicuous.

I certainly was not without resources in the situation. After all, I am a graduate of a Bible College with a number of years of pastoral experience behind me, and I certainly did know the *appropriate* way to give solace and comfort. It's a matter of putting your arm – *not arms* – around the shoulder of the person to be comforted, ever so properly, and then adjusting the distance between the two of you according to the seriousness of the problem. Above all, it is to be medicinal and impersonal. You are, after all, dispensing the appropriate dosage of care and concern while maintaining the appropriate distance which will assure both respect and respectability. So, while the other staff members did it their way, I did it the right way!

I was really rather proud of my ability to blend in with all these unusual and unexpected factors during the week of the first camp. I taught in the sessions assigned to me, and I prayed and counselled with young people as I felt it ought to be done. And all went quite well until the last day of the first camp at the Sunday morning communion service. It had been announced that there would be prayer for those who desired physical healing. It was suggested that the younger staff members who had been camping out with the young people during the week be the ones to pray with those who came forward for prayer, and so I was free to simply sit back and enjoy the service. I was doing just that, on the back row, when the young people went forward for prayer.

After the campers assembled for prayer, the minister in charge of that portion of the service looked up, caught my eye, and beckoned me forward. When I got to the front, he motioned me toward a young man kneeling alone near the communion table and indicated that he wanted me to pray with him. The only obstacle to doing so with ease was a row of folding chairs between the lad and me. I had at least two advantages over other staff members who might have been faced with the same situation. One was that I'm six feet four inches tall, and the other was that my system of theology required only that I 'lay hands on the sick'. Therefore, I got as close to the chairs as possible, stood on my tiptoes, and,

15

leaning over the chairs, I put my hand on his head and began to pray. I always pray with my eyes closed – simply a life-long habit learnt in childhood. But, for some reason I'm still not sure of, I opened my eyes during my rather soft-spoken prayer to discover that someone, trying to be helpful I'm sure, had quietly slipped the chairs out from under me while I was praying. I found myself suspended over space in a somewhat inglorious position steadying myself with my hand on the young man's head and with people seated directly behind me.

At that point, I did the most genteel thing I could think to do: I knelt down behind the lad and slipped my arm around his shoulder – in my fashion – and continued to pray. When he felt me slip my arm around his shoulder, he simply turned half-way round, put his legs out in front of him, and laid his head on my chest. I found myself with my arms full of a nineteen-year-old young man with a beard fuller than my own who was weeping, and I was extremely uncomfortable! I suppose that in that setting and after a week in that atmosphere it was a perfectly natural thing for him to do, but it wasn't natural for me, and I immediately changed the content of my prayer to explain to the Lord how uncomfortable I was and that this was none of my doing! I was just about to explain further to the Lord the abrupt departure I was contemplating when it occurred to me that it might not be a surprise to the Lord that I was in this situation and that he just might be in on the whole thing. I remember saying to the Lord, 'If you've got me here for a reason, you had better make it very clear very soon, because I don't intend to be here very long!'

It is difficult to put into words the events as they happened next. So much seemed to happen all at once. Suddenly, I wasn't embarrassed any more. I felt my arms tighten around the young man, and I rocked him gently, as I would have my own child. (My own son was actually just twenty years old at that time.) I felt as though warm oil were being poured over me, and I was suddenly very comfortable. Furthermore, I was aware that something of *me*, as opposed to a disembodied 'ministry' or some appropriate action, was going out to that young man. I felt that I knew what Jesus must have meant when he asked his disciples in the crowd, 'Who touched me? . . . for I perceive that virtue is gone out of me' (Luke 8: 45–6, AV). I had been a pastor for all those years, and I don't think a hard or unfeeling one, but I had never known anything like that before. I was also aware of something which has become the norm since that time, and that was that, however much I might have been doing for that lad in that moment of prayer, he was doing as much for me as well. Thus, the truth which I learnt in those first moments of renewal is that shared prayer and ministry is always two-way. One simply loses track of who's doing what for whom when the members of Christ's Body are truly caring for one another. I doubt that that young lad had any idea what was happening inside me, but my life was never again going to be the same.

Every day of the second camp was a new discovery. Deb and I would talk late into each night trying to understand what was happening – particularly to me. I read things in the Scriptures I had never read before, though I knew many of the passages by heart. I also discovered that some of the workers at Post Green had come there hurt and broken but were now functioning parts of the 'family' and ministry. Others had come there equally as disappointed with the typical church programme as I had been but had found new reasons for hope as they began to experience and take part in the renewal of the Church. As various ones began to share themselves with me, I became aware of a depth of healing and restoration which seemed to be directly related to the openness and the expressed love and affection amongst these people. It was a kind of healing I had never seen before through any mode of therapy or rigour of church attendance or involvement. The particular change which was taking place in me was an almost overwhelming love which I felt for many of the people in that situation. It was like meeting members of my family whom I'd never met before but somehow had always known. It was a little scary to feel such strong love for people who, by any external standard, were strangers whom I might never see again and who just might not feel for me what I was feeling for them. And, yet, any fears were swept away in what felt like torrents of love. Finally, I said to Deb, that if such a thing were happening anywhere on earth, I had to learn more about it and, if possible, be a part of it!

We returned to Southern California at the end of that summer and immediately began to ask the Lord to let us return to England and to Post Green, if that was his will for us. We began to tell our friends and family what we'd seen; or, just as often, they began to ask what had happened to us! One of our neighbours who had herself recently come into renewal even asked Deb if we were new converts. The responses to our enthusiasm and joy and the experiences we were sharing were mixed to say the least. Some of our friends, and some of the churches where we spoke, drank in everything we said. They couldn't hear enough about love, openness and honesty amongst the members of the Body of Christ, and people caring for one another. Others were frankly frightened by the prospect of letting anyone know them that well or come that close. Those months of sharing in a variety of churches and situations were our first encounter with the strange mixture which characterises the Church today. There are those whose hearts are open and longing for the new and the fresh and an end to pretence amongst God's children; and, at the other extreme, there are those who resist changes in the *status quo* with all the vigour of a crusader! We continue to find some ratio of this same mixture in nearly every church situation we encounter (including the newer groups which have been formed out of this current renewal for whom the *status quo* may be of only a few months' or years' duration).

As soon as we were sure that we were to be in England, life took on hectic proportions. Deb resigned her part-time teaching post, and I resigned from Whittier College. Never have resignations been written with more abandon. We sold our home and cars. Michele got married, and David settled into his last year of college. Our family and friends scarcely knew what to think of us as we said good-bye to them and to our former life-style. My behaviour seemed particularly strange to those who knew us best, since I'd always been extremely careful and cautious in matters of finance and security for the future. But I knew that, like Israel of old, I had been given the choice between life and death, and I was grabbing life with both hands.

Since my temperament, as well as occupation and training, fitted me best to be a teacher (even as a pastor my ministry and calling would have to have been described as teaching), it was natural for me to spend the following years at Post Green discovering the scriptural basis for a fullness of life through love and shared, open lives. The search for ways to share with the Church our corporate life and the

18

truths which God was showing us was a pursuit shared by all of us together at Post Green. The essential message which came out of our life together is that there is healing for broken lives and an on-going strength and fullness of life in loving relationships within the Body of Christ. Life isn't just an endurance test until heaven comes along to heal all earth's sorrows, but it can be rich in meaning and full of love. I must be careful to say, however, that the teaching contained in the following chapters is not intended to speak for Post Green; rather, it is simply my attempt to share those things which the Lord began to teach me during those years of shared life and ministry in the Post Green Community.

2. This is Man

Jesus said, 'The thief comes only to steal and kill and destroy; I came that they may have life, and have it abundantly' (John 10: 10). If we are ever to gain a clear understanding of these words of Christ, it is essential that we understand what it is in man which must be fulfilled in order for life to be 'abundant'. To know that, we must look rather carefully at man's nature to discover that which is truly 'natural' for him. But, before we can begin our discussion of man and his nature, there are several points which must be stated clearly.

First, I must say that my concern is for the individual and for the quality of his life. Abundant life is not some nebulous pattern of thinking which one struggles to achieve in some way; it consists of one's very state of being and the conditions under which one lives. Each one of us, as a child of God, can expect God to be working to bring us into full and abundant life. Such fullness of life includes all factors which make for health and wholeness. Furthermore, we must not understand these terms in any limited sense. True health and wholeness include the mental, emotional, and social aspects of man's nature, as well as his physical and spiritual needs. Therefore, whenever the terms *health* and *wholeness* are used, they will include all of these factors.

Second, we need to consider the relationship of the Church to abundant life. Just as God took care to provide both the garden and a helpmeet in order that the first man, Adam, might have that which he needed to live and be fulfilled, so he has designed the Church, the Body of Christ, such that redeemed man might be sustained and fulfilled upon the earth. But individuals do not relate in their daily lives to *The Church Universal*. Therefore, we must often refer to the local church body in which the individual functions as a 'member in particular' (1 Cor. 12: 27, AV). Thus, the terms *the Church* and *the Body of Christ* will refer to all true believers in Christ rather than any structure or movement, while the terms *the church* and *the body* will refer to local assemblies. It must be noted, however, that one is simply a reflection of the other; and, therefore, any quality of life which is appropriate for the Church should be equally present in the local church.

Finally, the main point of emphasis regarding the Church will be the current move of God's Spirit, by which new life, renewed life, is flooding into the Body of Christ throughout the whole of the Christian world. This move of the Spirit is called by various names depending upon the country in which it is happening and the church background of those who are experiencing it. The one term, however, which seems consistently to be heard is *renewal*. God, by his Spirit, is renewing his Church.

So much of what is written and shared about this current renewal is told in large and glowing terms, and rightly so. This must be one of the most exciting times in the whole of Church history! I can't begin to count the times I've walked in the fields or along the lanes in Dorset and thanked God that he has allowed me to be alive at a time like this, a time when love and care and openness are increasingly a part of life within the Body of Christ. While this move of the Spirit is referred to as a 'renewal of the Church', actually very little change is occurring in the institutions or structures within the existing Church. The real change is taking place as the Holy Spirit is renewing individual members of the Body. It is a renewed Church through a renewal of the lives and relationships which make up the Body. However, no change comes without tension, and drastic change can mean powerful tensions, and the changes characteristic of this renewal are often drastic! The changes have to do with established patterns of life; they require that we trust one another in new ways, make ourselves vulnerable in new ways, and risk new hurts on old scars.

This current renewal of the Church tends to involve consistently two major spiritual areas: (1) a renewed recognition of the person and power of the Holy Spirit at work in and through individual lives and (2) a renewing of love and loving relationships within the Body of Christ. Actually, it is this second aspect, the renewing of love with its power to heal and sustain fullness of life, which is the major theme of this book. If we are to appreciate fully the significance of the renewal at this time in human history, we must understand the relationship between man's basic nature and his need for

21

love – particularly as lived out in loving relationships – in order to be whole.

There can be little doubt that love and loving relationships are the sources of man's fullest joy and happiness, as well as his deepest hurt and sorrow. The longing for love and belonging along with the simultaneous fear of potential hurt and the loss of independence and individuality is a recurring theme throughout our society. That mixed theme is heard whether one turns to modern schools of philosophic thought or Hard Rock. It's the problem of *how to be free to go or stay as I please while being sure that there is always someone who cares whether I go or stay.* The psychoanalytic theory of Otto Rank is based almost entirely upon the idea that man struggles throughout the whole of his life with inner forces which need both union and dependency on the one hand and separation and individuality on the other.[1] If, then, we are going to suggest that love is the means to both fullness of life and the healing of life's deepest hurts, we are going to need to deal with man's basic fears which oppose both love and involvement. To do so, we will need to understand what it is about man's nature which requires love for survival and health while consistently fearing and rejecting it.

Let us turn, then, to the scriptural account of man's creation in order to gain as full an understanding as possible of his nature, of both his *need* for and *fear* of love. At this point, let me say that this rather formal study of certain facets of the nature of man created in the image of God is the most formidable subject with which we will deal. But, since it is the basic nature of man itself which provides the key to understanding full and abundant life, we must pursue as clear an understanding of his nature as possible.

The most fundamental fact which the Scriptures teach us about man is that he was made in the image of God, after his likeness (Gen. 1: 26). In principle, that fact alone requires that anything which is true of man's most basic nature must in some way be true of God. Therefore, we can learn a great deal about man by careful consideration of the pattern or blueprint from which he was constructed. This approach has an added advantage in that we are able to see these factors in God's nature without the contamination of the sin problem. Such a view helps us to glimpse the ideal toward which the Holy Spirit is directing us – particularly in this time of renewal.

There are two clearly documented facets of God's nature which, when taken together, help us see and understand more clearly man's inner struggles. These are God's self-sufficiency and his love. If we first trace the all-sufficiency of God, the picture which emerges is formidable indeed! When we listen to Elihu (Job's young friend) describe God, we see him 'clothed with terrible majesty' while he draws up the waters and pours them down again; we see the thunder and lightning declaring him, while he goes on doing all manner of 'great things which we cannot comprehend' (Job 36: 26–37: 24). Isaiah tells us, 'Behold, the LORD is riding on a swift cloud' (Isa. 19: 1). While in the first chapter of Genesis alone, there are recorded no fewer than fifteen separate acts of creation. There can be no doubt that our God is majestic in power and in creativity. Further, he is sufficient unto himself. The writer to the Hebrews records, 'For when God made a promise to Abraham, since he had no one greater by whom to swear, he swore by himself' (Heb. 6: 13). Also, when Moses questioned by what authority he was to say he had come to the people of Israel, God said, 'say . . . I AM has sent me to you' (Exod. 3: 13–15). Finally, he is capable of complete independence: 'Who has directed the Spirit of the LORD, or as his counsellor has instructed him? Whom did he consult for his enlightenment, and who taught him the path of justice, and taught him knowledge, and showed him the way of understanding?' (Isa. 40: 13–14). God, as he is thus described, could have few, if any, problems and certainly no lack of anything outside himself.

There is, however, another facet of God's nature equally well documented. John declares simply, 'God is love' (1 John 4: 16). Paul tells us that the mercy which man has received flows directly out of the 'great love with which he loved us' (Eph. 2: 4–7). This great love, focused upon man as it is, has through the ages caused God to make repeated overtures toward man and to ask for a response from him: '. . . call upon me in the day of trouble; I will deliver you' (Ps. 50: 15) or 'Come to me . . . and I will give you rest' (Matt. 11: 28). The psalmist declares, 'Enter his gates . . . and courts' (Ps. 100: 4); and James tells us, 'Draw near to God and he will draw near to you' (Jas. 4: 8). Isn't it incredible that, because he loves us, we're always welcome and are *never* an intrusion upon him.

I must point out that theologians want us to be sure to

understand that God's nature is such that there is no disunity or imbalance amongst his attributes and that all facets of his nature are in perfect harmony. While I'm sure that such is the case at some level, it is also true that a sort of 'hormonal balance' amongst God's various attributes does not solve all of his problems where man is concerned. The two facets of God's nature which we have described can clearly be seen to oppose each other as Moses and God talk over Israel's sin in making the golden calf. Moses tells God to either forgive Israel or blot Moses' name out of his book as well. God explains to Moses that 'whoever has sinned against me, him will I blot out of my book'. Surely that included Israel! Nevertheless, God follows Moses' counsel – he who needs no counsel from any man – but with the condition that he will at some point visit Israel's sin upon them (Exod. 32: 30–4).

A further example of this same dilemma is found in the sixth chapter of Genesis. Man has sinned and followed his own way until God is sorry that he made man and decides that he will destroy him and his immediate environment. But, then, God considers Noah. We have no scriptural reason to believe that Noah was so perfect that God could not be just in Noah's destruction along with the rest of mankind. The problem is not one of righteousness which Noah presents to God, but one which resides within God himself, within his love for man. God's justice and judgment and his love for man are simply not entirely compatible. Had God carried out his original intention to destroy all mankind, it would have been an entirely justifiable carriage of justice, and the problem of man and his sin would have been settled once and for all. But, because God acted out of love and grace where Noah was concerned and continued his love and patience toward mankind, it cost him Jesus.

While Jesus stands as the single greatest price which God the Father has paid for his continual effort to bring man to redemption, he is by no means the only price. The Scriptures are very clear about the personal hurt that God has sustained at the hands of man. The cries of the Old Testament prophets are filled with pleadings from God to man. The plea is for man to return to him so that he can heal their backsliding and prevent the destruction which is surely coming upon them. In one such instance, God pleads with Israel through the prophet Ezekiel: 'Say to them, As I live,

24

says the Lord GOD, I have no pleasure in the death of the wicked, but that the wicked turn from his way and live; turn back, turn back from your evil ways; for why will you die . . .?' (Ezek. 33: 11).

But perhaps the most poignant cry from God to Israel is recorded in the eleventh chapter of Hosea:

When Israel was a child, I loved him, and out of Egypt I called my son. The more I called them, the more they went from me; they kept sacrificing to the Baal, and burning incense to idols. Yet it was I who taught Ephraim to walk, I took them up in my arms; but they did not know that I healed them. I led them with cords of compassion, with bands of love, and I became to them as one who eases the yoke on their jaws, and I bent down to them and fed them. They shall return to the land of Egypt, and Assyria shall be their king, because they have refused to return to me. The sword shall rage against their cities, consume the bars of their gates, and devour them in their fortresses. My people are bent on turning away from me; so they are appointed to the yoke, and none shall remove it. How can I give you up, O Ephraim! How can I hand you over, O Israel! How can I make you like Admah! How can I treat you like Zeboiim! My heart recoils within me, my compassion grows warm and tender. I will not execute my fierce anger, I will not again destroy Ephraim for I am God and not man, the Holy One in your midst, and I will not come to destroy (Hos. 11: 1–9).

The most telling part of this revelation of God's heart toward Israel is his final declaration that, in spite of all the pain, he will continue to deal out of his love because the thought of his beloved Israel in ruins causes his heart to recoil and to turn warm and tender in compassion. The perfect balance between God's justice and self-sufficiency and his love may be such as to assure his integrity at all times, but it does not protect him from the pain and hurt of rejected love!

Now that we've seen the 'tug-of-war' within God where man is concerned, let's look at man fashioned in God's image. You don't have to look into the realms of philosophical discourse to discover the same ambivalence in man's nature – Pop music or Broadway will do. The Beatles cry out, 'Help! I need somebody', while Simon and Garfunkel declare, 'I Am a Rock' and then go on to tell us that love and friendship cause pain; therefore, it's better to be a rock because 'a rock feels no pain and an island never cries'. Broadway tells us: 'People who need people are the luckiest people in the world', while simultaneously declaring, 'I've Got to be Me' or expressing pride that throughout life 'I did it my way'. If we turn again to the Scriptures, we can trace the interwoven paths of man's self-sufficiency on the one hand and his need for love and interdependence on the other.

Unfortunately, the first two chapters of Genesis provide the only opportunity we have to see man's basic nature before the fall and the resulting contamination of sin. Those two chapters are enough, however, to give clear evidence of a creature created with certain power, creativity, and freedom of choice. God declares that he has given man dominion over various other creatures and particular vegetation for food and that man is to fill the earth and subdue it. A rather playful scene which depicts man's creativity is recorded in the latter part of chapter two as God has Adam name the animals. God is obviously not over concerned about Adam's ability to do those things assigned him; he is, after all, created in his Creator's image. It is the fact that Adam is made in God's own image which causes God to do something which he did not do at any previous stage of creation – he modifies the design! A creature designed after God's own image ought not to be alone: 'Then the LORD God said, "It is not good that the man should be alone; I will make him a helper fit for him."' It is very important to note that God's appraisal of man and his wellbeing occurs before the fall, at a time when man is in a genuinely sinless relationship with God. It is obvious, then, that God's concern for man is that he share life in relationships which are additional to his relationship with God, relationships which are necessary to the complete fulfilment of man's nature.

The distortion which sin has brought to both the nature of man and his state is impossible to comprehend fully; however, the same two facets of man's nature which we traced so clearly before the fall continue to be just as evident after the fall, albeit disfigured. The Scriptures continue a clear documentation of these two facets of man's nature; the same is true for man's secular history, as well as the more modern schools of personality and human behaviour. Examples of man's rather headstrong attempts to continue to exercise his dominion over the earth are plentiful throughout the annals of human history. As early in the scriptural record as the sixth chapter of Genesis, we find God's despair over man's motives and deeds in Noah's day: 'The LORD saw that the wickedness of man was great in the earth, and that every imagination of the thoughts of his heart was only evil continually. And the LORD was sorry that he had made man on the earth, and it grieved him to his heart' (Gen. 6: 5–6). Later the prophet Isaiah declares, 'All we like sheep have gone astray; we have turned everyone to his own way' (Isa. 53: 6). Returning to the eleventh chapter of Genesis, we find clear evidence of man's inventiveness as he plans and begins construction on the tower of Babel; but, again, it is an inventiveness bent upon separating him from God.

\Most current schools of psychology have some term or concept which accounts for behaviour which can best be described as 'self-assertive'. In Rank's theory it is labelled *counter-will*, while David McClelland has coined the term *achievement motive*. Robert White, who deals largely with childhood behaviour, speaks of the *effectance motive*. He describes the pleasure of 'the young child who takes delight in the sound it makes when he accidentally drops his rattle on the floor, and quickly learns to drop it regularly. And what even greater pleasure if the child can produce the additional effect of having an adult retrieve the rattle each time it is dropped!'[2] It is not that self-assertiveness is evil, in and of itself; on the contrary, it probably forms the basis for freedom of choice and the behaviour which we call choosing or 'free will'. But, if man's history is looked upon as a record of the choices he has made and carried out, then the wisdom in any man following only the dictates of his own heart is clearly questionable.

If we turn now to the question of love and loving relationships, the record after the fall makes it quite clear that man has also continued to need others (even if this need is frequently only acknowledged in a crisis). That man, however, is no more consistent and honourable in his expressions of love than in his stand for independence and self-sufficiency is also quite clearly recorded. Man's failure to sustain

27

healthy, loving relationships is true whether one is considering his relationship with God or his relationships with other men. Again, note God's despair over Israel: '. . . I am broken with their whorish heart, which hath departed from me' (Ezek. 6: 9, AV). And, if you take a short list from the Scriptures of man's relationships with others, you will find a full range which presents a strange mixture of both deep love and failures in love: Abraham and Sarah, Samson and Delilah, David and Jonathan, and the *same* David and Bathsheba. However inconsistent any of these relationships may have been or however out of touch with God's will some of them were, there can be no doubt that man continues to seek to express the loving, interdependent facet of his nature fashioned after the image of God.

We must consider another fact about man's need to love and be loved and to be sustained in human relationships. It is that this need is not limited to a single male-female union. We have tended, in Western culture, to limit the adult individual to one cross-sexed relationship in which to find all fulfilment of his need for love and intimacy. While it is true that the Genesis record of creation deals with a relationship which essentially is a marital one, the fourth chapter of Ecclesiastes is clearly speaking of a full range of relationships:

Two are better than one, because they have a good reward for their toil. For if they fall, one will lift up his fellow; but woe to him who is alone when he falls and has not another to lift him up. Again, if two lie together, they are warm; but how can one be warm alone? And though a man might prevail against one who is alone, two will withstand him. A threefold cord is not quickly broken (Eccles. 4: 9–12).

Further to this, Erich Fromm in his excellent book, *The Art of Loving*, points out that true love is an attitude which flows out of an individual to the world; whereas, the individual who is capable of loving only one other person often sees that other person as simply an extension of himself; or, just as often, the relationship is that of 'parasites' living in a mutually beneficial arrangement.[3] Finally, when we come to consider the Church in later chapters, we will see that the very living function of the Church, as well as the health of the individual members, depends on a wide range of relationships which are loving, open, and dependable.

If, then, man possesses the desire and inclination to express both his self-sufficiency (independence) and his love (interdependence), how is the apparent conflict between these two factors to be dealt with and settled? Again, it is most helpful if we look to the Original Pattern for our solution. What does God do relative to his self-sufficiency and his love? I think it would not be too great an oversimplification to say that the Scriptures are an extended history of God's postponing judgment while deferring to love. Peter, in speaking of God's coming judgment, says, 'The Lord is not slow about his promise as some count slowness, but is forbearing toward you, not wishing that any should perish, but that all should reach repentance' (2 Pet. 3: 9). As an overriding principle, God opts for love. The Scriptures are filled with the record of God's love for both individuals and peoples. We have already noted his mercy to Noah, his love for Moses, and his infinite love and patience for Israel. But, of course, the extension of God's love to all of us is most clearly seen in Jesus: 'For God so loved the world that he gave his only Son, that whoever believes in him should not perish but have eternal life' (John 3: 16). And Paul writes:

But God, who is rich in mercy, out of the great love with which he loved us, even when we were dead through our trespasses, made us alive together with Christ (by grace you have been saved), and raised us up with him, and made us sit with him in the heavenly places in Christ Jesus, that in the coming ages he might show the immeasurable riches of his grace in kindness toward us in Christ Jesus (Eph. 2: 4–7).

God is clearly aware of man's dilemma as a creature made after his own image, whose state is further complicated by the sin problem. And, thus, God has established laws to help man find peace to his soul, rest from his labour, and freedom from the ravages of sin. Please note that these laws are established for man's benefit and are not some sort of spiritual contortion into which God coaxes or coerces man! These laws are the most natural and the healthiest state in which man can live. When Jesus was challenged because his disciples picked grain on the sabbath, his reply was, 'The sabbath was made for man, not man for the sabbath' (Mark 2: 27). He had not come to bring man into more rigorous discipline but into abundant, everlasting life! Actually, God's laws are revealed throughout several hundred years of the history of his dealing with man in a variety of social and political settings. Thus, when Jesus was challenged by a Pharisee lawyer to state the most important or fundamental law, he replied, 'You shall love the Lord your God with all your heart, and with all your soul, and with all your mind. This is the great and first commandment. And the second is like it, You shall love your neighbour as yourself. On these two commandments depend all the law and the prophets' (Matt. 22: 37–40).

These fundamental laws of God flow directly from God's knowledge of man in his sinful state. Fallen man opts for self-sufficiency. He cuts himself off from God and others in his attempts to stand on his own; he strikes back and drives others away when he is hurt; and he is basically self-centred in his dealings with others. You will remember that God said, 'I am God and not man . . .I will not come to destroy' (Hos. 2: 9). God knows full well how man reacts in given situations, so he has given us laws to prevent us from bringing the pain and destructiveness of aloneness upon ourselves and from forcing the same hurt and pain upon others. It is for this reason that, for example, God has said, 'Vengeance is mine' (Rom. 12: 19). God simply cannot trust that man will deal lovingly and wisely with all parties concerned if he is allowed to pay back for injuries received! Therefore, God's laws require that man choose the ways of love which make possible the relationships which man needs for full and abundant life. God is also aware, however, that laws such as these, which require that man choose love and forfeit self-sufficiency, make man vulnerable to the same sorts of hurt which God himself has known in his love for man. Thus, he has made provision in the design and function of the Church for each member to be strengthened, cared for, and made whole. But, again, we deal more fully with this subject when we consider the Church in later chapters.

Let us return to Jesus' reply to the lawyer's question. It is important to note that Jesus did not actually answer the question as it was asked. The lawyer was, after all, undoubtedly schooled in the Greek tradition of thought and would have been accustomed to search for the 'single simplest element of truth'. Jesus' answer in effect is saying, 'It's not that simple; there are two irreducible laws: (1) *a right and loving relationship with God* and (2) *right and loving relationships with man.*' For hundreds of years now various factions of the Church, including modern Evangelicalism, have sought to skirt Jesus' answer and to return to the lawyer's stance that there surely is *one* most important law. As a result, the Church in certain quarters has had a long history of encouraging individuals to seek an ever closer and more rarefied relationship with God, while teaching them to look upon relationships with other human beings as a source of contamination to the primary one with God. Yet, God's word is clear that we cannot love God more than we love one another (1 John 4: 20–1) and that our love of the brethren is evidence of our own salvation (1 John 3: 14). On the other hand, we cannot love one another without God's love in us (1 John 4: 19). Thus, the two laws are inseparable; and, when anyone tries to elevate one above the other, the result is always a serious distortion of the purposes of God's law and a loss of the abundance of life and wholeness which are promised to those who wholly follow in the ways of the Lord.

It has, of course, been taken for granted in most Christian circles that fellow Christians ought at least to try to be friendly and get along reasonably well with one another. In the greater part of the Church, however, the spiritual emphasis has been almost totally upon the individual's relationship with the Lord. The result is a weak and ineffectual Church, almost unbearable loneliness, and a Church which knows practically nothing about how to experience love – much less how to teach and demonstrate it. It is largely this failure to see loving relationships within the Body of Christ as the vehicle for health for the individual and for evangelism which has rendered the Church so impotent at this particular time in man's social and political history. Therefore, as we consider the renewal of love within the Church, it is *loving relationships within the body*, rather than a generalised love, which will be the focus of concern. Throughout all of the discussion to follow, it, of course, is taken for granted that a healthy, loving relationship with God through Christ is accompanying all that is done or attempted in our relationships with others. If this is not the case, the result

31

will be a sort of 'Christianised humanism' (or social gospel) based solely upon good works and kindness. We seek in our love for him *and* for one another something far richer than either relationship on its own.

3. The World, the Church, and the John Wayne Syndrome

We have seen, then, that God's Word teaches that we must love and be loved in order to be whole and to fulfil our nature in his image. Furthermore, we have discussed the Church, the Body of Christ, as the intended setting for the loving relationships which we need. In light of these two factors, it is important that we look at the Church to see what means it provides for expressing love and for building the necessary loving relationships. While it is true that the current renewal is bringing marked changes in the area of love and care amongst the members, the fact is that most of us who grew up within the Church are not products of the renewed Church, but the old. Our values, habits, and personalities were shaped in a very conventional, reserved, and 'proper' atmosphere, where love and affection were concerned. As a result, even those of us who are the most excited by the new freedoms of the renewal are often faced with inner conflicts. We experience very mixed emotions as we attempt to learn to express our love more simply and to move into deeper relationships.

Furthermore, regardless of how influential the Church may have been in shaping some of our lives, the Church is by no means the only source of our values and ideals. Christianised Western culture, quite apart from the Church (or Christianity for that matter), has a fairly complex set of ideals, values, and traditions which are believed to provide the proper guidelines for a happy, moral, and productive life. More recently, many of these cultural ideals have been called into question as well. As individual Christians, then, we are faced with a renewal within the Church and a revolution in our society, both of which challenge many of our preconceived and previously unquestioned ideals. Certainly no area of our lives has been more challenged than that of our attitudes and ideals regarding love and interdependence.

If, then, we are faced with changing attitudes about love

and interdependence both within the Church and in the culture at large, it is vitally important that we carefully consider our own personal attitudes in this area. We must look to see where our attitudes have come from and upon what values they are based in order to be able properly to appraise and understand the impending changes. We must discover also how the Church renewal and the cultural revolution fit together. And what is more, each of us must finally decide whether to take our stand with the old or the new. In order to take stock of these issues, let's look in this chapter at our society and the Church in their more traditional state before the current questions and challenges; then, in chapters four and five, we will consider the culture in revolt and the Church in renewal and how these two movements are interrelated.

In order to trace the source of many of our personal values and ideas and to try to understand the current challenges to a good many of these, we will need to look rather closely at certain aspects of our culture. Before we do so, I would like to point out how important it is that we understand the social world of which we are a part. If we are to understand ourselves, we must know the ideas and ideals which have shaped our personal thinking and attitudes. And, if we are to understand our own generation to whom we offer the Gospel, we must know what has shaped, and is shaping, their ideals, their fears, their hopes, and their dreams; otherwise, our message may go unheard even by those who are yearning to hear it. Jesus certainly understood and spoke directly to his generation: 'But to what shall I compare this generation? It is like children sitting in the market places and calling to their playmates, "We piped to you, and you did not dance; we wailed, and you did not mourn." For John came neither eating nor drinking, and they say, "He has a demon"; the Son of man came eating and drinking, and they say, "Behold, a glutton and a drunkard, a friend of tax collectors and sinners!" Yet wisdom is justified by her deeds' (Matt. 11: 16–19). Jesus also knew and felt the mood of Jerusalem: 'O Jerusalem, Jerusalem, killing the prophets and stoning those who are sent to you! How often I would have gathered your children together as a hen gathers her brood under her wings, and you would not!' (Matt. 23: 37). These are only two examples from Jesus' ministry. He referred over and over again to 'this generation' in his teachings and warnings and even praise (Luke 16: 8). Without a doubt Jesus listened carefully to his generation; he knew it well, and he spoke to it honestly and directly. Can we do less as the stewards of God's message of love to our generation?

In chapter two, we considered the nature of man created in the image of God with the desire for self-sufficiency and independence on the one hand and the desire for love and interdependence on the other. If we try to evaluate the moral guidelines which Western culture has established for human behaviour, what we discover is that it is the self-sufficiency and independence side of man's nature which has been emphasised as the Western ideal. In Britain, that ideal is referred to as the *stiff upper lip*; and, in America, it is known as the *John Wayne syndrome*. It all means the same thing: 'I can stand on my own two feet, thank you very much'; 'I can take care of myself'; and 'even if I can't, you'll be the last to know!'

Just when and how such an emphasis started is a little difficult to trace, but Trevelyan says: '. . . the real strength and felicity of the Victorian age lay . . . in the self-discipline and self-reliance of the individual Englishman, derived indeed from many sources, but to a large extent sprung from Puritan traditions to which the Wesleyan and Evangelical movements had given another lease of life.'[1] In the mid-Victorian era, Samuel Smiles wrote a book and started a movement both of which were entitled *Self-Help.*[2] The ideal which emerged was that the individual could do and become anything he set his mind on, if he would simply tap in on his inner resources and never give up!

Even the briefest glimpse at the poetry which grew out of that Victorian ideal is most revealing. Rudyard Kipling's poem, 'If' contains nineteen conditions such as:

' If you can meet with Triumph and Disaster
    And treat those two impostors just the same . . .

Or,

    If you can force your heart and nerve and sinew
        To serve your turn long after they are gone,
    And so hold on when there is nothing in you
        Except the Will which says to them: 'Hold on!'

35

Or, particularly,

> If neither foes nor loving friends can hurt you,
>> If all men count with you, but none too much . . .

Then, says Kipling to the young man,

> Yours is the Earth and everything that's in it,
>> And – which is more – you'll be a Man, my Son![3]

Edgar A. Guest wrote one poem which declares, 'It couldn't be done . . . and he did it',[4] and another which begins, 'Stick to it, boy'.[5] Sarah K. Bolton admonishes us to 'Paddle Your Own Canoe',[6] and Phoebe Carey, in terms reminiscent of the English ideal, instructs us to 'Keep a Stiff Upper Lip':

> There has something gone wrong,
>> My brave boy, it appears,
> For I see your proud struggle
>> To keep back the tears.
> That is right; when you cannot
>> Give trouble the slip,
> Then bear it, still keeping
>> A stiff upper lip!

> Though you cannot escape
>> Disappointment and care,
> There's one thing you can do, –
>> It is, learn how to bear.
> If when for life's prizes
>> You're running, you trip,
> Get up, start again,
>> Keep a stiff upper lip!

> Let your hands and your conscience
>> Be honest and clean;
> Scorn to touch or to think
>> Of the thing that is mean;
> But hold on to the pure
>> And the right with firm grip;
> And though hard be the task,
>> Keep a stiff upper lip!

Through childhood, through manhood,
  Through life to the end,
Struggle bravely and stand
  By your colors, my friend;
Only yield when you must,
  Never give up the ship,
But fight on to the last
  With a stiff upper lip.[7]

All of this emphasis upon individual strength and inner resource meant that any suggestion of softness, weakness, or dependence had to be carefully stamped out; and Western society began to raise generation after generation which were increasingly ashamed of anything that wasn't evidence of strength. Thus, J. B. Watson, the American psychologist who introduced Behaviorism in 1913, saw programmed training as a means to rear children who could face the hostile world, and mothers were admonished not to destroy the effects of this 'proper' training by tenderness and affection:

> Mothers just don't know, when they kiss their children and pick them up and rock them, caress them and jiggle them upon their knee, that they are slowly building up a human being totally unable to cope with the world it must later live in ... There is a sensible way of treating children. Treat them as though they were young adults ... Never hug or kiss them, never let them sit on your lap. If you must, kiss them once on the forehead when they say goodnight ... Can't a mother train herself to substitute a kindly word, a smile, in all of her dealings with the child, for the kiss and the hug, the pickup and the coddling? ... If you haven't a nurse and cannot leave the child, put it out in the backyard a large part of the day. Build a fence around the yard so that you are sure no harm can come to it. Do this from the time it is born ... If your heart is too tender and you must watch the child, make yourself a peephole so that you can see it without being seen, or use a periscope ... Finally, learn not to talk in endearing and coddling terms.[8]

While this view was never popular in its extreme, it certainly reflects the ideal of individual strength and self-reliance to combat life; and, from that time on, many techniques and texts for child rearing clearly embody such a general attitude. (Note also the idea that *adult* behaviour does not include hugs and kisses!)

Furthermore, we cannot ignore the influence of world history. There can be little doubt that two major wars within twenty-five years have played a significant role in creating the *he-man ideal*. Most nations in the Western world have been forced to think in terms of self-protection, and many have continued to keep standing armies throughout times of peace as well as war. As a result, the past several generations have lived in constant awareness that a large part of the male population had to be suitable for military duties. Perhaps, then, it is not too surprising to find that such traits as gentleness and sentimentality are not only undervalued but actually feared at such times in world history. While few parents have gone as far as Watson's advice quoted earlier, the attempt to produce manliness has led to some rather incredible extremes. If a little boy hurts himself and begins to cry, it's not too unusual, even now, to hear Mum or Dad hush his crying by telling him to 'be a big boy' or that 'men don't cry' – never mind that he's only eighteen months old!

In terms of man's nature as we've discussed it, this extreme he-man ideal has been achieved by the almost complete denial of the need for love and affection. While there are those who will defend the ideal of the strong, independent individual on a variety of grounds, the cost of such an ideal cannot be denied – a cost borne by both the individual and society. We have produced several generations of males who are embarrassed by their own feelings of gentleness and tenderness. While such men may be efficient at business, hard work, and defending their country, thousands of homes have been robbed of a gentle, loving, and lovable husband and father. Furthermore, we've made men so afraid of their own need to be affectionate that meaningful relationships with other adult males is almost impossible. Thus, we have created the he-man role and isolation and loneliness in one fell swoop.

It is important to note, however, that the demands of self-sufficiency and efficiency are not demands which our culture has made upon males only. The adult woman in our society is expected to cope with the home, children, husband, and often a job outside the home as well – and to do so nearly singlehandedly without complaint or exhaustion! It's no wonder that our mental hospitals are filled with both men and women who have simply opted out and that our medical hospitals are filled with those whose illnesses are basically emotional. It's a strange set of values which makes mental and emotional illness preferable to interdependent relationships in which people love and support one another without shame or reproach.

During this time, the Church, too, became an advocate of the John Wayne syndrome – but with one major difference. It was assumed that the individual was not sufficient in himself and that he would need the help of the Lord in order to be a real he-man! Much of the preaching and teaching, as well as the books which were written, promised the individual Christian that, if he would just learn a certain way to pray, or adopt a particular attitude toward life or adversity, or be faithful to various religious practices, he could single-handedly enter into a realm of constant, victorious Christian living. Most Christians simply assumed that such he-man Christianity was possible – in fact should be the norm – and that it only required a little more diligence on their part to 'get there'.

The sort of scriptures which were emphasised during this period of Church history were those which admonished: 'be strong in the Lord' (Eph. 6: 10) or 'I can do all things through Christ which strengtheneth me' (Phil. 4: 13, AV). Often, there was very little attention given to the context from which such scriptures were taken, and it was certainly not considered that such promises, encouragements, or instructions could have been intended for the body of Christians collectively. Our cultural blinkers caused us to interpret nearly all scriptural instruction as though it were dictated from God directly to the *individual* believer. As a result, more and more, the only relationship which really mattered was between the individual and the Lord. All other relationships were seen as secondary and inferior; they seemed to have little, if any, spiritual merit.

As a matter of fact, in this atmosphere of spiritual individuality, believers were warned to trust the Lord alone and to beware of human involvement. Such scriptures as Jeremiah 17: 5–8, which warns against trusting in the arm of flesh, were interpreted to mean that human relationships were dangerous and that the only true friend or companion a man could have was the Lord and, furthermore, that God himself said so! Thus, Christian friends, and even one's husband or wife, became potential threats to the quality of the individual's spiritual well-being, if they were loved or trusted too much. (We will look at Jer. 17: 5–8 again in chapter eight when we consider relationships in the Body of Christ.)

Even the concept of love itself had to be redefined in order to allow the individual to love others without getting too close or too involved with them. Such a redefinition is made possible by categorising various 'types' of love according to the Greek terms for love which are used in the original New Testament writings. The two most significant terms in setting up this system of thought are *agape* and *phileo*: *Phileo* expresses friendship, brotherly love, or emotional affection; *Agape* expresses a divine love which includes a commitment and a genuine concern for the welfare of the loved one and, according to Vine,[9] is an act of will rather than feelings. Thus, *agape* is held to be the superior love and *phileo* to be the inferior. The implication would seem to be clear: As Christians, we should love the Lord and one another with *agape* love. That way, we can love rationally, as an act of will, and can express our love in acts of concern which do not require deep emotional feelings or involvement, particularly in human relationships. This explanation and redefinition continue to be the classical Evangelical teaching on New Testament love. And what is more, such rational, non-emotional love fits comfortably within the John Wayne syndrome and does not disturb the he-man image, whether one is the giver or the receiver of such love.

The extent to which this classical redefinition of love distorts God's intentions can best be seen if we stop now and consider another way to understand the Greek terms for love as they are used in the New Testament. First of all, it must be pointed out that Greek is not God's native tongue! It is a language of men. It is the Greek language, not God, which divides love into these particular types and categories. Furthermore, *agape* love was known and talked about by ancient Greeks long before Christianity; therefore, there is no spiritual halo around the term itself. But, what is most important for our consideration is the fact that the New Testament usage of the terms does not fall into the neat categories that some would suggest. The New Testament writers used the terms interchangeably in describing or referring to the same relationship. Both *agape* and *phileo* are used to express God's love for man (John 14: 21 and John 16: 27) and the Father's love for the Son (John 3: 35 and John 5: 20). Furthermore, both terms are used to direct Christans to love God (Luke 10: 27 and 1 Cor. 16: 22) and to love one another (Gal. 6: 10 and Titus 3: 15). The most obvious reason for such mixed usage is that true love involves the elements which are signified by both terms; and, thus, both terms are necessary to convey the full extent of love which God intends in any truly loving relationship.

The most often quoted interaction between the two terms, *agape* and *phileo*, is found when Jesus and Peter meet after Christ's resurrection (John 21: 15–17). Jesus asks Peter three times if he loves him (*agape, agape, phileo*). The classic explanation is that Jesus uses the 'superior' term the first two times; but, at Peter's insistence on the 'lower' term, Jesus finally and reluctantly drops down to Peter's level of love. Actually, Peter uses the more specific and affectionate term, *phileo*, each time. He felt his love for Jesus deeply, and he told him so.[10] However, as the idea that *agape* is the superior love came to be applied to Christian relationships in general, it came to be accepted that this highest form of love was not only possible but actually enhanced by a certain aloofness and limited involvement with others, except on a 'higher' or 'more spiritual' plane. And warm, tender, 'emotional' *phileo* love came to be seen as unnecessary and even suspect relative to the more rational, non-emotional commitment of *agape*.

Thus, the Christian was encouraged to stand on his own two feet – with the help of the Lord. He was warned against the dangers of trusting other human beings, and he was taught a sort of love which could be accomplished as an act of will, whether he felt it or not. And with that, the stage was set for the same isolation and loneliness within the Church as was true for the society at large. But, as a matter of fact, the problem was often even worse for the believer. He professed that Jesus was all that he needed for complete happiness and stability. If his upper lip trembled, it was a reflection not only upon himself but upon the Lord! Therefore, it was equally as necessary to play the role before one's fellow Christians as it was before the outside world. There simply was no place to be real and honest about one's fears or heartaches or what it feels like to be a human being who's a Christian. The Church, thus, became a contributor to the problem of alienation and loneliness in modern society rather than the solution.[11]

At that point in time, churches were often little more than a collection of individual believers each one living out his own relationship with the Lord. The solution for their human problems was to read the Bible *more*, pray *more*, and get *more* involved in the church programme, which usually included some sort of 'evangelism' or at least an attempt to build larger attendances which was often interpreted as 'the furthering of the Gospel'. While all the statements about the Church prior to renewal are written in the past tense as though they described a closed page in Church history, for many Christians in many churches these statements are still a fairly accurate description of current Christian life and teaching. Furthermore, many of these issues are by no means totally resolved within those bodies which are experiencing renewal; however, a commitment to openness and honesty within the renewal offers real hope for a growing expression of man's need to love and be loved. New wine is being poured out, and individual believers and whole church congregations are moving into new dimensions of spiritual life and loving relationships.

The renewal of the Church is coming at a time in world history when the old attitudes of individuality and self-sufficiency are being challenged at every level of human society. There can be little doubt that God is preparing the Church to speak to a new generation. It is this new generation and the renewed Church which I would like us to consider in the next two chapters.

4. The Culture in Revolt

Historians, as well as social scientists, will undoubtedly be trying to unravel the causes and effects of the current cultural revolution for a very long time to come. While it is true that ideas and ideals typically change from generation to generation and create differences of attitude and opinion which can be described as 'the generation gap', the changes over the last thirty years have often created not only gaps but great gulfs between the succeeding generations. Parents who were unquestioningly secure in their ideals and values were suddenly faced with children who did not share those ideals at all, children whose manner of dress and hairstyle were often a source of embarrassment to both their parents and society. But beneath these more superficial changes lie far more fundamental differences. Often, one senses a new gentleness and affection and a regard for the worth of other human beings which lends itself far better to care and concern for common human interests than to competition and the drive to scramble to the top of the heap at any cost.

I'm sure that we are much too close in time to evaluate many of the changes or to sort out accurately causes and effects. All we can hope to do is to discuss several of the areas of change, or at least evidence of the desire for change, so that we may be better prepared to hear and understand the heart cry of this new generation. For only after we have heard and understood that cry, to which God himself is responding, can we understand the significance of the unique features of the current renewal within the Church.

The stiff upper lip, with its requirement of individual strength, is an unbearable task master. It requires that we maintain self-control at all times and that we appear calm and unruffled on the outside no matter how much we may be troubled within. Thus, we develop masks to wear in various social settings to help us hide our fears, uncertainties, and embarrassment. In the late fifties, social psychologist Erving Goffman published a theory of social behaviour based entirely on the idea that we perform the whole of our public

43

life as though we were 'on stage' and carefully conceal the true 'backstage' self.[1] About the same time, however, there were those who were beginning to say, 'Let's try dropping the masks – just a little, and let's see if we can be real.' Special times and places were set up for being honest. Sensitivity and encounter groups began to form at most major universities and colleges, as well as in industry. The purpose of these groups was to provide a place for feelings to be shared openly and honestly rather than being hidden behind polite conversation as they typically are. Even special retreat centres (such as Synanon in California) were established where groups could meet for extended periods of time in an attempt to discover better ways for people to communicate with one another. In an attempt to make people aware of the basic deceit in typical social relationships, Eric Berne, MD, published *Games People Play* in 1964. In it, he defines seven categories of games which typify life in our culture and then goes on to plead for a life-style beyond games.[2]

In the same year as *Games People Play* appeared, Sidney M. Jourard published *The Transparent Self* in which he envisions an honest society in which marriages and family, friendships, education, and even illnesses can be experienced and shared openly without deceit. In the preface to the first edition, Dr Jourard warns: 'We camouflage our true being before others to protect ourselves against criticism or rejection. This protection comes at a steep price. When we are not truly known by the other people in our lives, we are misunderstood. When we are misunderstood, especially by family and friends, we join the "lonely crowd". Worse, when we succeed in hiding our being from others, we tend to lose touch with our real selves. This loss of self contributes to illness in its myriad forms.'[3]

The price we pay for the masks we wear is loneliness. Isn't it strange that we live at a time in world history when the earth is more populated, even over-populated, than ever before. And yet in the Western world, loneliness is one of the most serious problems facing us. How tragic that, as medical science is extending the average life expectancy, what we're being offered is added years of loneliness. While solutions to loneliness are not coming quickly or easily, nearly every sector of our society seems to be aware of the problem. John Lennon and Paul McCartney sing about 'Eleanor Rigby' who,

. . . picks up the rice in a church where
a wedding has been, lives in a dream,
waits at the window, wearing the face
that she keeps in a jar by the door,
who is it for?

The song then asks two questions which are a commentary on our time:

all the lonely people, where do they
all come from?
. . . where do they all belong?[4]

Sociologists and psychologists, as well as those in many other social sciences, have turned a great deal of attention toward exposing the problem of, and seeking solutions to loneliness. Just a few examples will serve to illustrate their growing concern. As early as 1941, Erich Fromm's *Escape From Freedom* dealt with man's fears of alienation and recommended that we needed to learn to deal with others in relationships of emotional intimacy.[5] In 1950, David Reisman and his colleagues published *The Lonely Crowd* which emphasises the sense of aloneness in modern society.[6] Frieda Fromm-Reichmann published an article on loneliness in 1959 in which she says, 'Loneliness seems to be such a painful, frightening experience that people will do practically anything to avoid it.' She then goes on to challenge psychiatrists and psychologists to seek ways to understand the problem better.[7] In the late sixties, psychiatrist William Schofield spoke to a different facet of the problem. In his book, *Psychotherapy: The Purchase of Friendship,* he points out that in our present social state people often turn to professionals to buy a sort of open, honest friendship which is missing from their lives, even when they have both family and 'friends'.[8] These examples are only a token of the hundreds of research projects, articles, and books which represent the attempt of the scientific community to expose and deal with loneliness in modern Western society.

City planners and social architects have also attacked the problem of isolation and loneliness. Their 'solution' has been to design and build modern, high-rise 'centres of community living'. But such planned housing units have often

45

been found to create even more loneliness than the types of housing which they sought to replace. Loneliness simply isn't dispelled by the mere physical nearness of other human beings; loneliness has to do with the person hidden inside, behind the masks. The real barriers between people are not determined by physical distance alone nor are they built of brick and mortar; they are made of social roles, games, and the accumulated deceit of years of the stiff upper lip. These more recent attempts to combine the answer to urban housing problems and loneliness and isolation have proved to be rather costly mistakes in both money and human suffering. And yet, they are at least witness to the growing concern to do something about the 'lonely crowd'.

While it is gratifying to see these more professional concerns for our self-imposed loneliness, it is the growing willingness to take off the masks and to begin to admit to one another our need for love and friendship which finally offers a new hope. In one of the most honest pieces of poetry I know, James Kavanaugh asks:

Will you be my friend?
There are so many reasons why you never should:
I'm sometimes sullen, often shy, acutely sensitive,
My fear erupts as anger, I find it hard to give,
I talk about myself when I'm afraid
And often spend a day without anything to say.
   But I will make you laugh
   And love you quite a bit
   And hold you when you're sad.
I cry a little almost every day
Because I'm more caring than the strangers ever know,
And, if at times, I show my tender side
(The soft and warmer part I hide)
   I wonder,
   Will you be my friend?
A friend
   Who far beyond the feebleness of any vow or tie
   Will touch the secret place where I am really I,
   To know the pain of lips that plead and eyes that weep,
   Who will not run away when you find me in the street
   Alone and lying mangled by my quota of defeats
   But will stop and stay – to tell me of another day
   When I was beautiful.

Will you be my friend?
There are so many reasons why you never should:
Often I'm too serious, seldom predictably the same,
Sometimes I'm cold and distant, probably I'll always change.
I bluster and brag, seek attention like a child,
I brood and pout, my anger can be wild,
    But I will make you laugh
    And love you quite a bit
    And be near when you're afraid.
I shake a little almost every day
Because I'm more frightened than the strangers ever know
And if at times I show my trembling side
(The anxious, fearful part I hide)
    I wonder,
    Will you be my friend?
A friend
    Who, when I fear your closeness, feels me push away
    And stubbornly will stay to share what's left on such a
      day,
    Who, when no one knows my name or calls me on the
      phone,
    When there's no concern for me – what I have or
      haven't done—
    And those I've helped and counted on have, oh so
      deftly, run,
    Who, when there's nothing left but me, stripped of
      charm and subtlety,
    Will nonetheless remain.

Will you be my friend?
    For no reason that I know
    Except I want you so.[9]

In reply to the poet's unashamed question, 'Will you be my friend?', an equally unembarrassed answer comes:

When you're weary, feeling small,
    When tears are in your eyes, I'll dry them all;
I'm on your side.
    . . . If you need a friend . . . Like a bridge over troubled
    water
I will lay me down.[10]

There can be little doubt that we're moving into a new era of openness and honesty where our need for one another is concerned. Admittedly, cultural revolutions do not transform a whole society overnight, and we still have a very long way to go, but we're moving!

The desire to drop the masks and the willingness to admit to and deal with our loneliness are amongst the more obvious effects of the cultural revolution. An even more fundamental change has to do with our attitudes toward love itself – and particularly toward affection. Again, the social scientists have spoken out 'loud and clear'. In the late fifties and throughout the sixties, psychologist Harry F. Harlow published his work on the nature of love. If we recall the advice given to mothers by J. B. Watson which was quoted in chapter three, the full impact of Harlow's findings will be better appreciated. His research was done with Rhesus monkeys. Infant monkeys were raised in a variety of situations: some with their natural mothers, some with a wire frame 'mother' from which milk was dispensed, and some with the same sort of wire frame 'mother' which was covered with towelling in order to provide contact comfort. In some studies, the infants were allowed access to other infants; in other studies, they were isolated with their particular sort of 'mother'. The results have been very clear. If the infant is deprived of intimate contact comfort with something or someone, he will fail to develop normal social behaviour, and the effects will be seen in nearly every sphere of adult life. Furthermore, Harlow found that even survival itself was less likely when the infant was deprived of the needed bodily contact.[11] The same result was found by Rene Spitz, MD, who reported in 1945 that human infants who are deprived of handling over a long period of time will tend at length to sink into an irreversible decline and are far more likely to die from otherwise minor illnesses.[12] Far from a thing to be avoided, as Watson suggested, touching, handling, and other forms of affectionate behaviour are essential to proper development and, for that matter, life itself!

Infants and children who grow up in a 'non-touch' culture become adults with all manner of fears and hang-ups where affection and intimacy are concerned. Children find hugs and kisses natural and joyous; but, after persistent moulding into cultural patterns, as adults, they feel strained and awkward to hold hands, caress, or even to give or receive a gentle pat on the hand or cheek. Such cultural shaping of behaviour means that we unwittingly train-out the very aspect of our nature from which the fullest joys and deepest healings come.

It isn't possible to consider even a fair representation of all of the books and articles currently available on the subject of the loss of love and intimacy in our culture. But, even the briefest consideration of a few examples is most revealing. In *The Art of Loving*, Erich Fromm suggests the need to practise the art of being a loving person and discusses the fears which surround love: '. . . while one is consciously afraid of not being loved, the real, though usually unconscious fear is that of loving. To love means to commit oneself without guarantee, to give oneself completely in the hope that our love will produce love in the loved person. Love is an act of faith, whoever is of little faith is also of little love.'[13] That theme is dealt with more fully in *The Risk of Loving* by Simons and Reidy who strongly encourage us to take whatever risks are involved in loving.[14] In reading the many books on love, one is forced to the same conclusion again and again: we can either love and risk being hurt or not love and be sick!

Intimate Behaviour, by zoologist Desmond Morris, deals with man's need to touch and be touched. Morris concludes that the human, when not warped by his civilisation, is fundamentally endowed with a great potential for tenderness and intimacy.[15] *The Greening of America*, by Charles A. Reich, deals with the history of America in terms of three definite ideals which have emerged. The first was 'The Rugged Individualist', the second 'The Corporate Roleplayer', and the third which emerged in the mid-sixties is so new that no label is readily available. It is the ideal of the new generation. This new ideal values the acceptance and worth of all human beings – including one's self. It especially values liberation which frees the individual to be himself.[16] Finally, just the titles of two recent text books in social psychology will give an indication of the extent to which students are being made aware of the human need for love and tenderness: *Emotional Intimacy: Overlooked Requirement for Survival*, by Alan M. Dahms,[17] and *Liking and Loving: An Invitation to Social Psychology*, by Zick Rubin.[18]

Another sign of the revolution in our culture is the large number of dissidents who from time to time form into groups or movements of many sorts. While many of these groups are not defensible nor are all of their causes justifiable, the fact remains that many of the individuals who have 'dropped out' of the mainstream of Western life have done so in an honest effort to find a simpler life-style where more emphasis is placed upon care and concern for one another than upon material possessions and social status.

Various labels have been applied to some of the more noticeable groups or movements: Hippies, Yippies, Flower Children, etc. They have championed a variety of causes from world-wide peace to civil rights to non-competitive communal living. While many people from a more conventional stance have tended to write off these groups as consisting of unreliable individuals who simply want to opt out of their rightful share of social duty, there can be little doubt that at the base of many of these movements there is a deeply felt conviction that there simply must be viable alternatives to wars and killings, hunger and disease, and the sort of inequality which leads to vast wealth on the one hand and crushing poverty on the other. Their insights, as well as their hopes and aspirations, are reflected in such folk-style music as: 'Where Have All The Flowers Gone', 'We shall Overcome', 'The Family of Man', and 'If I Had A Hammer'. Implicit in all of these is the underlying belief that in love we will find the solution to the 'lonely crowd' and to man's injustice to man.

Many of those who have dropped out of the mainstream of Western living have moved into various communal life-styles in an attempt to find fulfilment for those basic human needs which they believe to be denied, or at least minimised, in modern Western culture. Rosabeth M. Kanter, in *Commitment and Community*, states, '. . . communal ventures represent not only alternatives to life in the dominant culture but also attempts to realise unique ideals, dreams, and aspirations.'[19] In the past, few utopian-styled communities have survived the test of time; in spite of this historic evidence, the past fifteen years have seen the emergence of widespread interest in such life-styles. Literally hundreds of communities with varying forms of living styles have come into being. Obviously, many people would rather risk the

50

strong possibility of a utopian failure – while seeking to fulfil their ideals and dreams in a shared venture – than to face the even surer prospects of loneliness and isolation in a world where individuals are required to stand on their own and to vie with one another for a place to stand.

Finally, let's look at the changing face of social roles, particularly masculine and feminine roles. The feminist movement is perhaps the loudest and most extreme voice which has been heard regarding social expectations. The movement is militant in its protest against the previously unquestioned social guidelines laid down for the life-style and behaviour of women. While many will deplore the entire idea of a feminist revolt, there can be little doubt that, more and more, women are taking their place alongside men in nearly every sector of our society. While I'm not attempting any value judgment at this point, I would like to make one observation regarding the feminists' objectives. My concern is that they often seem to be setting their sights on the wrong objective where acceptable role behaviour is concerned. Rather than seeking acceptance for tough, aggressive, success-orientated behaviour for women, every effort should be made to bring the roles for women *and* men closer together somewhere nearer the centre of the spectrum. The feminists ought to be as concerned for the liberation from the pressures of unnatural expectations for the men in our culture as they are for the liberation of the female. Otherwise, we could begin to see female, as well as male, embodiments of the John Wayne syndrome, and that prospect is both frightening and mind boggling!

There is evidence, however, that the John Wayne syndrome may not continue to provide the ideal for men in our culture. While the dissenting voices are not as many nor as loud as those which champion the feminist cause, they are beginning to be heard. A recent book, *The Hazards of Being Male* by H. Goldberg, discusses many of the problems which surround the he-man image. While I disagree with various ideas, conclusions, and recommendations contained in the book, one of the most significant chapters makes a plea for the return of 'The Lost Art of Buddyship'. It is pointed out that, once an adult male in our society marries, he is not only cut off from close relationships with adult females other than his wife but also other males, because continued friendship with other males is considered an

51

immature hang-over from adolescence or, even worse, an indication of homosexuality.[20] Thus, the married male has been typically limited to the single close relationship with his wife for the whole of his adult life in order to be considered both mature and normal.

Another part of the he-man image which has come under recent attack is the idea that men are by nature not as emotional as women. We have held for a very long time the idea that men are not as sentimental and do not 'feel' as deeply as women. Sidney M. Jourard, in *The Transparent Self*, takes issue with this entire attitude about men. It may be true that men in our culture appear to be tough, objective, achieving, and generally emotionally unexpressive; however, 'seeming is not being'. Dr Jourard also reports that it has been found that men reveal less about themselves in conversation than women do. Again, we have been taught to believe that *real* men keep things to themselves; and, therefore, it is supposed that men do not need to talk about themselves. However, research evidence is expected soon which will relate the amount a person is open, in terms of self-disclosure, to the proneness to illness and even early death. It is, then, entirely possible that social expectations where masculinity is concerned have not only robbed males of the variety and richness of emotional expression but have actually contributed to their shorter life expectancy as compared to women.[21]

Again, however, it is not the social scientists alone who are raising their voices in protest. The following poem by James Kavanaugh pleads in the most poignant way for love and acceptance for boys, and the men they are to become, for being just what they are rather than forcing them to pretend in order to be loved:

I knew this skinny little kid
  Who never wanted to play tackle football at all
But thought he'd better if he wanted
  His daddy to love him and to prove his courage
And things like that.
  I remember him holding his breath
And closing his eyes
  And throwing a block into a guy twice his size,
Proving he was brave enough to be loved, and crying
  softly

Because his tailbone hurt
And his shoes were so big they made him stumble.

I knew this skinny little kid
   With sky-blue eyes and soft brown hair
Who liked cattails and pussy willows,
   Sumac huts and sassafras,
Who liked chestnuts and pine cones and oily walnuts,
   Lurking foxes and rabbits munching lilies,
Secret caves and moss around the roots of oaks,
   Beavers and muskrats and gawking herons.
And I wonder what he would have been
   If someone had loved him for
Just following the fawns and building waterfalls
   And watching the white rats have babies.
I wonder what he would have been
   If he hadn't played tackle football at all.[22]

One of the latest developments in the creation of a new masculine image is the television series *Starsky and Hutch*. The show depicts two fast, tough cops who work together on special assignments in the greater Los Angeles area. The thing, however, which makes these two policemen different is the relationship between them. In an interview reported in a London evening newspaper, Aaron Spelling, the 'father' of the show, stated, 'We are not afraid to admit it, Starsky and Hutch are allowed to love each other. One is wounded, the other holds him in his arms. Real tears are shed.' The executive co-ordinator of the company which makes the show said, 'Starsky and Hutch are not just two strong, virile guys, but virile guys who care deeply about each other, show affection and the warmth that mature men, secure in their own masculinity are not afraid to display.'[23]

It is, however, the television audiences' acceptance of the show which is the most revealing in terms of a new, more affectionate masculine ideal. In London, the show has hit the top of the ratings, and what is even more significant is that the highest-rated episodes are the ones in which Starsky and Hutch take each other into their arms and hold one another in moments of warmth and caring.[24] It seems clear, then, that there are many in our culture who are looking with acceptance and longing at this new image of masculinity, even if only in the privacy of their own living room.

53

At this point, I would like to say that I have intentionally dealt almost exclusively with changes in the masculine role. This is not because I am unaware of the need for change in the feminine role as well but because my concern is primarily for the human need for love, particularly affection, and the need to express our more tender feelings; and whatever the feminine role in Western culture may lack or however much it may need to be modified, it has always allowed women far more latitude in expressing and receiving affection and tenderness than men. I have, therefore, limited the discussion, rather than consider other issues which are outside the scope of this book and which are being dealt with widely by others.

Finally, it must be pointed out that, throughout all of the discussion of various changes or evidence of the desire for change within our culture, I have made no attempt to evaluate or judge the merits of any ideal, group, or point of view; rather, I have simply attempted to show the culture in transition. The direction of the transition is away from stark individualism toward a more gentle, caring concern for human worth. In terms of our definition of the nature of man, this transition is a shift away from independent self-reliance toward love and interdependence. As such, it is a shift which brings man's ideals nearer to God's solution to man's inner conflict which we discussed in chapter two. However, it must be remembered that man, without God, is no more successful in his attempts to give and receive love than in his attempts to be self-reliant. Man simply was not created to function – even in loving relationships with others – independent of God. We will be looking in chapter seven at the Church as it has been designed by God to provide the setting for healthy, natural life – for interdependent, loving relationships with both God and man. Before we consider the ideal Church, however, let's look at the present day Church in transition; let's look at the Church in the process of being renewed.

5. The Church in Renewal

Just as cultural revolutions do not transform a whole society overnight, Church renewals do not transform the Church, or churches, instantaneously! Thus, as we consider some of the changes in practices and attitudes within the Church, what we see very often are just the signs of a new mood or emphasis within a limited sector of the Church. Sometimes, the signs of renewal are seen in bold relief against the backdrop of the old. Perhaps more often, however, the only real evidence of renewal is a more honest recognition of the complexity of the problems facing our society and the Church. Nevertheless, one cannot deny the presence of the new wine, and in this lies the hope that we will be able to make ourselves heard by this our generation and by the same means find healing and new meaning for our own lives.

The current renewal of the Church seems to have started sometime in the mid-fifties. Those of us who were well encapsulated within our own denominations began to hear rather 'strange stories' about things which were supposedly happening in the old-line, historic churches. I must confess that we Pentecostals did not give much credence to those stories. We had had a corner on the market where such things as healing and 'speaking with other tongues' were concerned for a very long time. It seemed rather unlikely that much would happen within denominations and movements which had so clearly turned away from these things in the past. But the stories persisted; and, in time, shortly after my return to higher education, I met my first 'Spirit-filled Episcopalian'. Her name was Jean Stone, and she had founded the *Blessed Trinity Society* which at that time published a magazine called *Trinity*. She referred to 'the charismatic movement' which, at that time, was both a new term and a new idea to me. Furthermore, it was obvious that she and the others I met who were part of the movement were not out of the Holiness tradition which is so characteristic of many branches of the Pentecostal movement. Their attitude toward such things as smoking and a 'before dinner drink' made it obvious that, if they were receiving all the blessings from the Lord which they claimed, God was certainly not playing by the rules! Looking back, one could scarcely have foreseen all that was coming. Actually, it was several years later – after the Jesus People[1] with their impact on the drug scene, the charismatic outpouring in the Roman Catholic church,[2] and the emergence of thousands of home-based, interdenominational prayer groups – that the full impact of what God was doing by his Spirit began to be more evident. (We will be discussing the importance of small groups within the Church in later chapters.)

As we saw in chapter two, this renewal tends to fall into two broad categories. One is a renewed appreciation for the person, power, and ministry of the Holy Spirit. Thus, in every place where the renewal is occurring, there is a renewed expectancy on the part of believers in terms of answered prayer and more dynamic Christian living. The other category is a renewal of love amongst believers. Somehow, the Holy Spirit is breaking through the barriers and masks, and true affection and honesty are marking the relationships amongst the members of Christ's Body. It is this second category, having to do with love and loving relationships, which is particularly significant in relation to the revolution in our culture. What we are experiencing is God restoring the Church and reminding the Church of some of the forgotten lessons in loving and being loved in order that we might be both individually and collectively healed from the wounds of a stern, unfeeling, and often loveless past and, in our healing, hear and speak to this new generation.

Before we look at some of the particular dynamics involved in the current renewal, let's consider how this renewal relates to the person and ministry of Jesus. It is essential that we see this relationship, since whatever happens in the Church must have its roots and pattern in Christ, or it doesn't belong in the Church in any age. The ministry of Jesus has always been definable in at least two categories: that to *unbelievers* and that to *believers*. Mark refers very clearly to this distinction: 'In fact, he taught only by illustrations in his public teaching, but afterwards, when he was alone with his disciples, he would explain his meaning to them' (Mark 4: 34, The Living Bible). More recently, I have become aware of another distinction in Christ's ministry: that to *individuals* and that to *groups*. If one puts these

56

various distinctions together, the result is four categories: *individual unbelievers, individual believers, groups of unbelievers*, and *groups of believers*. Let's briefly consider examples in each of these categories.

INDIVIDUAL UNBELIEVERS: The rich young ruler comes immediately to mind (Matt. 19: 16–22). 'If you would be perfect, go, sell what you possess and give to the poor, and you will have treasure in heaven; and come, follow me.' Obviously, this instruction and invitation are not universal teachings to all who seek Christ. These words were tailored to that young man. Mary, Martha, and Lazarus no doubt owned property, but their property seems to have provided hospitality and care for Christ. In one case, possessions were a deterrent to following Jesus wholly; and, in the other, they were the very expression of love and care for him. Another clear example of tailoring to the individual is found if we compare Christ's response to the Samaritan woman at the well (John 4: 4–42) to his response to the woman taken in adultery (John 8: 3–11). When Jesus dealt with the adulterous Samaritan woman who sought to engage him in theological debate, he became her accuser in order to reveal himself to her. But, when he dealt with the woman taken in adultery who was surrounded by accusers, he became her defender, again, in order to reveal himself. Note: When Christ gave himself to an individual, he moved right in to deal with that individual where he was. He loved *the person – then* and *there*!

INDIVIDUAL BELIEVERS: My favourite example here is Jesus talking to Peter after his resurrection (John 21: 1–19). 'Simon, son of John, do you love me?' He asked him the question that any of us might ask if we loved someone dearly and something had come between the two of us: 'Peter, still love me?' It is the relationship, and the hurt, between them which fills those words with such poignant meaning. Such searching, tender words as these come only to one of his own.

GROUPS OF UNBELIEVERS: Much of Christ's public ministry falls into this category, although he did teach his disciples 'publicly' as in the case of the Sermon on the Mount (Matt. 5: 1). But certainly the first teaching of the parable of the sower was to a great crowd that had gathered (Matt. 13: 1–9).

GROUPS OF BELIEVERS: The second teaching of the

parable of the sower is a clear case in point (Matt. 13: 18–23). Another example is the questions which Jesus put to his disciples: 'Who do people say that I am?' and 'But who do you say that I am?' It was in response to these questions that Peter declared, 'You are the Christ, the Son of the living God' (Matt. 16: 13–20 and Luke 9: 18–21). Such questions as these were never shouted to the unbelieving crowd. They were reserved for those to whom the Holy Spirit was revealing the truth about Christ and his kingdom.

The church for many past generations has concentrated on the *group* ministry of Jesus. We have measured our successes and failures in terms of the colossal. We've filled the largest tents, halls, and arenas in the name of evangelism. We've built our church buildings to house a 'spectator sport' where neat rows of people *observe* that which is happening 'up front'. In the typical church setting, the nearest thing to you as you sit in the pew is very often the back of the head of the person in front of you. While no one can discount the ministry of the mighty preachers who shaped that era, nor the fruitfulness of the evangelism of those years, such an approach to the Gospel only fulfils half of Christ's ministry. It is true that he often preached to great multitudes; but, just as often, he gave himself freely to those such as Nicodemus, Zacchaeus, and the woman at the well. He was so incredibly available to individuals. This current renewal is marked by the Holy Spirit teaching the Body of Christ how once again to give themselves to each other and how to speak from one heart to another, outside the Church as well as within.

But to learn these lessons means that we in the Church have to come to grips with the problems which our own values and backgrounds create as we seek to relate on a more open, honest, personal level. Since the Church is largely made up of people whose thinking and personality have been shaped by Western ideals and since the Church itself for a very long time helped to support those same ideals of strong individualism, it is not too surprising to find the same areas of problem and change in the Church which we identified in the culture at large. Furthermore, it is when we see what God is doing in the Church in these same areas that it becomes apparent just how much God is fitting the Church to speak to this new generation.[3]

Masks are often worn to church with even more diligence

than to other social functions. They are all the more un-yielding because they have been fashioned and sanctioned by various scripturally based teachings. For example, we are admonished in Paul's writings against doing anything which would cause our brother to stumble. These scriptures, when interpreted in teaching and preaching, are often seen to mean that I must, therefore, always appear as an en-couragement to my brother. And when that idea gets in-terpreted in terms of 'John Wayne Christianity', it comes to mean that I must never appear weak or discouraged but, rather, must always inspire my brother to stand strong. In order to do that, I create a 'super-spiritual' mask which implies that I always feel strong in the Lord so that my brother will be encouraged, and not discouraged, by me. The irony is that often it is my apparent unwavering strength which is the very source of my brother's dis-couragement with himself. He knows that he feels weak and alone sometimes, but he doesn't want to let on lest he should be a source of discouragement to me, so he bravely pretends so as not to discourage me, while I'm pretending so as to encourage him! No doubt an entire catalogue could be am-assed of the 'games Christians play' in their attempt to appear to be what they aspire to be.

Perhaps the greatest loss to the individual believer, be-cause we play such games, is in terms of the mutual care which Christians are supposed to have for one another. The admonition to bear one another's burdens implies that we will know about each other's problems. Actually, in our shared life in the Post Green Community, we found over and over again that, far from being dragged down, fellow Christians greatly benefited by sharing failings, heartaches, and even broken dreams with one another. Honesty is so refreshing and so healing! Such honesty means that my brother and I can stand together to believe God for his promises in our shared life, and that is an undeniable scrip-tural pattern for strength! (Eccles. 4: 9–12).

Voices are certainly being raised within the Church, plead-ing for a new day of honesty and mutual understanding amongst Christians. John Powell, of the Society of Jesus, in his book, *Why Am I Afraid To Tell You Who I Am?*, says, 'None of us wants to be a fraud or to live a lie; none of us wants to be a sham, a phony, but the fears that we experi-ence and the risks that honest self-communication would involve seem so intense to us that seeking refuge in our roles, masks, and games becomes an almost natural reflex action.'[4] Paul Tournier, the noted Christian psychiatrist, adds, 'Listen to all the conversations of our world, between nations as well as those between couples. They are for the most part dialogues of the deaf.'

In *Why Do Christians Break Down?*, William A. Miller discusses many of the false and unrealistic expectations under which Christians labour as they attempt to live out Christian principles. The preface to the chapter entitled 'False Faces' says, 'Why do I break down? I break down because I feel the need to present myself as something other than I believe I really am, and the pressure to keep up the front and play the role is just too much.'[5]

In the Church (just as in the larger society), it is not only those trained in the social sciences who are raising their voices against deceit amongst people. Gordon Bailey has published three small volumes of poetry: *Plastic World*, *Moth-balled Religion*, and *Patchwork Quill*. Above everything else, his poetry pleads for honesty within the Church. In the introduction to the second volume, he says, 'In a world where young people, possibly more than ever before, demand to know the Truth, I simply plead, along with many others, for an end to sham, pretence, hypocrisy, and all things counterfeit.'[6]

The sort of release and joyous relief which can be known when we begin to let the masks drop is expressed beautifully by Graham Kendrick in his song, 'My True Feelings':

> I'm a novice, when it comes to being honest about my
>   feelings . . .
>   Please excuse me, I've spent so many lonely years
>   locked up inside me . . .
> But my confidence in friends is really growing
>   And I'm not half so scared to make my feelings
>   known . . .
> Now I can laugh and I can cry and I can sing
>   The sweetest joys and saddest tears can now begin
> An honest heart and honest eyes it's been a beautiful
>   surprise
>   Since God gave me my true feelings.[7]

It is obvious that a new day of openness and honesty is

coming in the Church. Little by little the masks are coming down. It's not easy for any of us as we begin to express our deeper feelings and honest ideas; but, each time our further revelation of ourself is met by acceptance and love, we're encouraged to take the next step. One thing we must guard against, however, is that we don't relegate openness and honesty to certain times and places. We noted in chapter four that psychology's answer to the cry for honest acceptance has been to form sensitivity and encounter groups or even to set up special retreat centres where people can meet for honest encounter. What a tragic and frustrating state of affairs – to live at a time when one must make an appointment to be honest! If only the Church will be bold enough to yield to the leading of the Holy Spirit at this time, we have the opportunity to create a wholly new, honest lifestyle. We have the opportunity to offer not only moments of honest encounter but a life of openness, honesty, and love. And such a way of life is a commodity which is almost extinct upon the earth!

The Church, too, pays for its masks and roles in loneliness. Church roles, with their accompanying masks, are many and varied: the mask of the clergyman fashioned to meet super-human expectations, the mask of the faithful Christian fashioned to meet ideals of individual strength, self-imposed masks fashioned to hide embarrassment or guilt. The list of masks is endless, but their consequences are uniform – loneliness. But, thank God, the Church is increasingly aware of the problem. Billy Graham and Paul Tournier have both named loneliness as the most devastating problem facing us today. Graham Kendrick's song, 'Loneliness', reminds the Church that:

> Loneliness is a common thing
> For people who've done something wrong enough
> To never have the courage to admit it
> To even their closest companions in life.[8]

How tragic that the Church should have allowed itself to be overcome by the very problem to which it needs to be speaking. If ever there was a time when the rebuke 'physician heal thyself' was appropriate, it is now!

But the Holy Spirit is stirring the Church. The problem of loneliness is being talked about openly. Marion L.

61

Jacobsen's book, *Crowded Pews and Lonely People*, pinpoints many of the sources of loneliness in typical church life and suggests many practical measures which can be taken by local church bodies to combat the problem of loneliness within their fellowship.[9] Furthermore, many groups are doing more than just talking about it. In the attempt to deal with loneliness and aloneness on very practical levels, many churches and Christian groups are providing informal meeting places and even temporary living accommodation where people can get together. Whether these places to meet take the form of a coffee house for young people, a sharing meeting over tea and cakes, or half-way houses where ex-addicts live together in order to support one another, they all point to a renewed conviction that 'it is not good for man to be alone ...'

When we hear the poet ask the question, 'Will you be my friend?', and we hear the answer come back, '... if you need a friend I'm sailing right behind ... like a bridge over troubled water I will ease your mind', it's rather easy to get caught up in sentimentality and to feel that the world really is becoming a better place. And, to the extent that a more truthful presentation of ourselves is a step toward health, the world certainly is moving toward a healthier approach to human life in general. But, again, the Church has a unique opportunity. We can offer more than friendship to the lonely; we can offer family – loving, dependable, open, honest family. We haven't got such relationships in large supply right now, but we are moving in that direction, and it is happening. How strange that such a statement should seem bold. We've called ourselves brothers and sisters for such a long time, but how lightly we've taken those labels. Yet, thank God, all over the world there are Christians who are coming to share their lives with one another in very tender, loving and practical ways. They are building relationships which are based on love and the realisation that God has caused them to belong to one another. I'm not talking about a sort of comradeship or group identification; I'm talking about two people loving each other and being dear to one another in ways which are reminiscent of Paul and Timothy's or David and Jonathan's love for each other. When love such as that exists and is available within the Body of Christ on a grand scale, we'll have a renewed Church indeed – a Church where loneliness has no place!

But before that day can come, or even dawn, we'll have to deal honestly and courageously with our fears of love. One of the major reasons that the classic explanation of *agape* versus *phileo* love has been so popular in the Church is that an emphasis upon *agape* love allows us to love without being *in* love and keeps love on a more business-like basis. (See chapter three for the discussion on *agape* and *phileo* love.) But, if by love we mean something that we feel and take sustenance from, then we face real fears. The most basic fear where such love is concerned is, of course, related to our very nature. If we choose the way of love, we have to choose against independence and self-reliance. We get involved with one another; we come to need others as well as be needed by them, and that can be very frightening. Furthermore, we're almost certain to get hurt, since the other humans with whom we have loving relationships are themselves imperfect and capable of being just as selfish or thoughtless as we are at times. And what is more, if we're truly open with those we love, they make inroads into our private world. We have to explain or justify ourselves and be willing to change if our behaviour, ideas, or attitudes are not justifiable or are hurtful to others. These are all 'risks of loving'. And at some point, with all of these factors taken honestly into consideration, each one of us must make the decision as to whether or not love is worth it. God's example, advice, and law direct us to choose love – not a blind, romanticised choice but a choice thoughtfully made with our eyes and our heart wide open – but we must choose.

Just as in the other areas of renewal, the Holy Spirit is speaking to the Church through a variety of voices. John Powell's book, *Why Am I Afraid to Love?*, deals with many issues involved in our fear of love. Thankfully, there is no attempt to gloss over the costs in an effort to make love more appealing: 'Love . . . is a self-donation which may prove to be an altar of sacrifice . . . Because of the inward pains that all of us bear, the scar tissues that are part of our human inheritance, because of the competition and example of a self-grasping world, it will be difficult for us to make the sacrifice of ourselves that is involved in loving. Loving always means at least this sacrifice . . .'[10] The very idea of giving ourselves away or losing ourselves, or even our rights, often seems both risky and foolish. It is, therefore, wise to remind ourselves of certain principles in God's Word: 'One man gives freely, yet grows all the richer; another withholds what he should give, and only suffers want' (Prov. 11: 24). Certainly, God's ways are not man's ways.

In chapter one, I pointed out that psychologists and clergymen alike are typically trained to keep a 'proper' social distance from their clients or parishioners. It was one of the most revolutionary discoveries for me to find that more healing took place in someone who came to me in trouble when I felt and showed love and affection than when I remained professionally detached. I was, therefore, encouraged when I read *Love Therapy*, by Paul D. Morris, which sets forth an entire therapeutic system based upon love and involvement.[11] Thank God there are places where the troubled Christian can find love, as well as counsel. While there will always be those who need the specialised ministry of trained counsellors, one looks forward to the day, as the Church opens to love and loving relationships, when there will be less need for the Christian to 'purchase his Christian friendship' from the professionals within the Church.

Again, the clergy and counsellors within the Church are not the only voices pleading for love amongst Christians. John Witmer, when at Wheaton College, wrote these lines:

> you followers of the Bearded Christ
> and you of the Carpenter
> and you of the Twelve-year Philosopher
> withhold your talk at Easter-Christmasers
>   you back-rowers, and morning onlys
>   and 5 days of chapel already.
> fighters for ecumenical support of Indian Bill 12
> unprejudiced suburbanite who's never eaten chili
> seekers of Truth and Life and The Way,
> PLEASE LISTEN!
> when you
> retreat from your Crusades
> and pull back from your Causes
> and finally have time for somebody,
> have time for me;
> I need somebody to love me.[12]

It's a strange irony that the world is more readily accepting expressions and displays of affection than the Church. Starsky and Hutch can now hold one another in their arms for all the world to see, and the television audience begs for more; while in most churches, a quick, rather embarrassed handshake is the extent of the tenderness that one will see. Yet, it is the Church which has operated for *two thousand years* under the instruction: 'By this all men will know that you are my disciples, if you have love for one another' (John 13: 35). Apparently, Jesus assumed that his followers would so love one another that the world would witness that love. The irony becomes tragic when we realise that, because of embarrassment and false ideals, we are hiding from the world the very thing for which they are longing and which will speak to them most powerfully of Jesus. As a result of our failure, our generation now turns to the pretence of television rather than to the Church to see love and affection.

Thank God this lack of affection is not true in the whole of the Church. There are many fellowships where love abounds! The Jesus People and a host of informal fellowships, as well as renewed churches around the world, provide believers with tender love and affection and make available an unashamed witness of that love at which the world can warm their hands and their hearts. Again, the Church has such an advantage over the society at large, if only we will exercise our options. The make-believe world of Starsky and Hutch fades when the television goes off; but, in those fellowships of believers where love is a way of life, the world is able not only to look in at that love but to come in and to share in it. Furthermore, those who come in and choose to stay can become part of a family where hearts, hands, and lives are joined in love.

In chapter four, we discussed the commune movement and suggested that communes were often made up of people who have given up on society and dropped out in protest. I'm not sure that the same can be said by and large of those who form Christian communities. Very often such communities have been formed in an effort to try to speak to both the Church and to the society. If that is protest, then I think it must be at least acknowledged that it is a loving protest in an effort to find and share alternatives to the *status quo*. In addition, many Christians are retaining traditional life-styles while forming into home fellowships or cell groups within larger church bodies in an effort to find more intimate fellowship in which they can find and give love and support. While such small, loving groups are not communes at all, they certainly embody the spirit of community amongst their members.[13] It was in regard to this spirit of loving support for one another that Dietrich Bonhoeffer wrote *Life Together* in which he suggests guidelines for Christian fellowship and reminds us 'how inexhaustible are the riches that open up for those who by God's will are privileged to live in the daily fellowship of life with other Christians'.[14]

While small, informal cell groups are far more numerous, organised communities which involve commitment and life-style are also a growing part of the Church renewal.[15] As such, they provide a setting in which basic Christian principles may be lived out and a regular, daily sharing of life which more typical life-styles do not permit. Stephen B. Clark is co-ordinator of the Word of God Christian Community in Ann Arbor, Michigan. In his book, *Building Christian Communities*, he defines the basic Christian community as: 'An environment of Christians which can provide for the basic needs of its members to live the Christian life.' He also points out that it is essential that the interaction between members be relationship-oriented and not just task-orientated.[16] (We will return to the relative importance of relationships over task when we discuss the Church more fully in chapter seven.)

Before leaving the subject of Christian communities, however, I would like to speak from my own experience of living and working as a part of the Post Green Community for two and a half years. Because communities differ so widely, there is a temptation to indulge in careful descriptions in order to justify oneself and to forestall criticism from those who are unsympathetic toward such movements. Rather than attempt any such justification, however, let me simply relate some of the benefits of living in community. One of the most obvious benefits is the opportunity to share life every day with other Christians and to apply the scriptural principles of sharing a common life in everyday situations. Another is the opportunity to build loving, deep relationships which involve sharing oneself and one's goods with others. There is, also, the healing for past wounds which flows from these deep relationships. And there is the learning to give of *oneself* as part of any caring ministry rather than offering skills or knowledge only. Further, clergy are basically taught how to lead and minister alone. What a joy it is to learn how to share with others even the simplest acts of formal ministry so that at all times the 'body' is functioning rather than any one member. And, finally, I would want to add that loving relationships within community allow others to get close enough so that their love can bring about fundamental changes in one's life and personality. That dynamic for change is not perfect; community members are no more perfect than other Christians; but, when we are loved for what we are and not for pretence, there is very real healing which allows growth and change.

Having listed many of the benefits which I personally found in Christian community, I must say that I'm confident that the community setting is not the only place where such benefits are to be found. The principles which we learnt together in community are certainly appropriate for any body of believers. It must be honestly said, however, that few local churches are designed to allow, or are prepared to help, their members to involve themselves as deeply with one another as is required to bring about the sort of shared life which I have been describing. Furthermore, it must be said that no church programme or schedule of private devotion will bring about such changes in individual lives. The only vehicle for such change is loving, committed, interdependent relationships within the Body of Christ.

Finally, let's consider changes in attitudes relative to sex-role expectations. There are clear signs of such changes within the Church, as well as the larger society. Recently, two major church bodies in America and Canada joined the growing number of denominations and fellowships to ordain women with full clergy status, and there is every reason to believe that others will soon follow suit. While there are church leaders of equal rank and devotion on either side of the issue, and those who are opposed are very firm in their conviction, it seems very likely that women will more and more take a place alongside men in positions of authority within the Church. It is not my intention to get involved in doctrinal controversy; however, perhaps we do need to remind ourselves of at least one brief scriptural statement. We are told that 'in the last days . . . I will pour

67

out my Spirit upon all flesh, and your sons and your daughters shall prophesy . . . yea, and on my menservants and my maidservants in those days I will pour out my Spirit; and they shall prophesy' (Acts 2: 17–18). With such promises as these at stake, we must be very careful that we do not close our ears or our minds to the voice of the Lord as he speaks to his Body – whether the vessel he chooses is male or female.[17]

As we consider the prospects of women members of the clergy, I would plead the same cause as when we considered masculine and feminine roles in the culture at large. We must not seek to place women into the present role of the clergy. Rather, we must make every effort to allow members of the clergy, whether male or female, to live openly with their problems and needs. No calling or task within the Body of Christ should ever cut off any member of the body from the loving care of the other members. As long as we prescribe a role for clergy which does not allow them the same margin of error and the same need for open, honest love and care as the other members of the body, we force upon them an unbearable loneliness and isolation which is contrary to every scriptural principle.

Let us look, also, at the changing attitude toward the ideal masculine role within the Church. At this point, we have only a suggestion of change, but the suggestion is there. Perhaps the single most influential group in the Church in this regard has been the Jesus People. Anyone who sees these young people together can't fail to be impressed by the tender, loving affection amongst them. How good it is to see two young men throw their arms around each other in simple love for one another and for the Lord. But this is only a small segment of the Church; one will find no such signs of affection in most fellowships. Isn't it ironic that nearly every goal in an English football game is followed by hugs all round for the lad who scores the goal. Yet, nothing that God or man could do would warrant such a simple expression of affection or gratitude in most churches.

The reluctance on the part of males to have or express love for one another within the Church is even more difficult to understand if one considers the examples of loving relationships in the Scriptures. David and Jonathan loved each other and pledged themselves to one another. Their love was such that when Jonathan died David said:

How I weep for you, my brother Jonathan;
How much I loved you!
And your love for me was deeper
Than the love of women!
(2 Sam. 1: 26, The Living Bible).

Jesus' relationship with John was such that John referred to himself as the 'disciple whom Jesus loved'. And Paul's letters to Timothy begin 'my dearly beloved son'. There can be little doubt that these were relationships of genuine love and that the love was expressed; David and Jonathan as well as Paul and Timothy wept when apart from one another. (We shall return to the subject of love and affection within the Body of Christ in chapter seven.)

In many ways, the renewal has just begun. The new ways and ideas which we have been discussing have yet to begin in most local churches. But, wherever the Gospel is being preached, there are signs of the renewal. It is true – God is pouring out his Spirit on all flesh. As we noted in chapter two, however, this is a renewal of individual lives and of relationships rather than church governments and structures. Therefore, as we continue to consider both the blessings and the problems of renewal, it is, essentially, the cost to the individual which must be calculated. The renewal of the Church is only as powerful and pervasive as there are individuals being renewed. It is, therefore, to the individual in renewal that I would like us to turn next.

6. The Cost of Renewal is Change

So far, we have talked about the renewal in the Church in terms of its overall effect on various ideals, attitudes, and teachings as well as on the less structured way in which many fellowships and ministries are conducted. But this renewal is not general; it is specific. The Holy Spirit is transforming individual lives, fashioning them anew in order that they might be whole and be able to speak with renewed conviction and relevance to this generation. In chapters three and five, we looked at the Church before this current renewal and in the midst of renewal. Even the briefest comparison of the Church before and during the renewal suggests many areas of change, changes which challenge all sorts of cherished ideals and attitudes and even our individual social roles and self-image. These are changes which, if incorporated honestly into our lives, leave us very different people. Thus, the cost of renewal is change – deep, irreversible, personal change.

Jesus said, '. . . which of you, desiring to build a tower, does not first sit down and count the cost, whether he has enough to complete it? Otherwise, when he has laid a foundation, and is not able to finish, all who see it begin to mock him, saying, "This man began to build, and was not able to finish." Or what king, going to encounter another king in war, will not sit down first and take counsel whether he is able with ten thousand to meet him who comes against him with twenty thousand? And if not, while the other is yet a great way off, he sends an embassy and asks terms of peace. So therefore, whoever of you does not renounce all that he has cannot be my disciple' (Luke 14: 25–33). He had just told the multitude that anyone who wanted to be his disciple would need to be prepared to turn his back on his family and home and to bear his own cross; in fact, he would need to renounce all that he had. How strange those words must have sounded to good, law-keeping Jews. One certainly didn't need to do any of those things to be a good Jew, and a good Jew was exactly what God wanted a man to be. Their social structure, their law, even many of their traditions had come directly from God himself. How could anyone say that there was a better way to relate to God; yet Jesus was saying to them that they would need to be prepared for very real changes from the *status quo* and that they, therefore, needed to count honestly the personal cost of those changes.

Change is always particularly difficult for those who are successfully established in a given social structure before it begins to be threatened by the very challenge to change. For the Jew in Jesus' day, the challenge was not a new or different religion; it was a new relationship to Jehovah through Jesus Christ and a renewal of the spirit of the law as opposed to the letter of the law. The change, then, was not from error to truth or evil to good but from veiled truth to a fuller truth and from good to better. And so it is in the current renewal of the Church. The old ways are very often defensible in terms of the historical setting in which they flourished. They have often served the Church well. What the Holy Spirit is showing us now is that there are new, better ways or that there are forgotten ways which need renewing. Many of us find it as difficult to believe that there could be better ways than those we cherish as the Jews in Jesus' day found it.

We of the English-speaking world are particularly proud of our spiritual heritage. Historically, our nations have sought diligently to spread the Gospel to the corners of the earth. Under our various structures of government, Christianity and Christian churches have prospered influentially and materially. We, therefore, consider it an affront to be told that there are better ways than we have already found or devised to relate to God or to our fellow man.

My mother's mother lived in our family home throughout all of my childhood. She had been a church-going Christian all her life, and she really didn't understand too well when my mother and father were 'converted' and started going to the new 'Pentecostal' church in town. But she did want to go to church, and that's the church to which the family car went every Sunday; therefore, so did she. Now we were taught a very clear definition of the conversion experience and even as children were taught to be on the alert for any unconverted person we might meet. It was, therefore, inevitable that it should come to my attention that my grandmother never said that she was 'saved', and I decided that I needed

71

to do something about that! One day I said to her, 'Grandma, are you a Christian?' She looked at me as though I had lost my mind, and she said, 'Of course I'm a Christian – I'm an American.' And that was that! As a church-going citizen of 'Christian America' she was exactly what God wanted a person to be. (I'm pleased to say, however, that my grandmother's definition of Christian did change before the end of her life as she came to know Christ as Saviour and Lord.)

As regards religious tradition, the Jew in Jesus' day and the Christian of our day have much in common. Both have strong cultural heritages in terms of a knowledge of God. Both have had their values and ideals shaped by a social tradition which itself has strong religious overtones; both have difficulty imagining a better way than the traditional; and both find the challenge of change difficult and frightening, if not outright heresy. It is because of these similarities between those to whom Jesus spoke and Christians of our day that it is appropriate for us to consider the lives of those who followed Jesus as we attempt to assess the changes which can be expected in the life of the individual when he becomes a living part of this renewal. A careful look at some of the changes, and their cost, in the lives of first-century Christians will help us each to count the cost of change in our own life.

Before we go on to consider individuals and particular changes in their lives, I would like to clarify one point. Throughout this book, I am speaking to the issue of personal renewal in the life of the believer. It is assumed that the individual already knows Christ and has a living relationship with him. I am well aware, however, that in the course of this renewal many who have been simply nominal members of Christian churches, as well as others who have had no previous experience with Christ, are coming to know Christ as Saviour and Lord and are coming into the renewed Church simultaneously. Though these newly converted individuals may not have the same problems as the well-entrenched believer with long-standing, active church affiliation, the cost of their renewal is paid for in the same commodity – change – change which is often radical both in relation to church tradition and to social custom.

Relative to the *extent* of personal change, Jesus said, 'Neither is new wine put into old wineskins; if it is, the skins burst, and the wine is spilled, and the skins are destroyed; but new wine is put into fresh wineskins, and so both are preserved' (Matt. 9: 17). Our concern, then, is with 'new-issue wineskins', whether the individual has known Christ before or not. The new wine will force new shapes and dimensions and only new or *renewed* wineskins will do. With this in mind, let's turn now to a consideration of the lives of some of the first-century Christians in order better to appraise the cost of personal renewal.

As a psychologist, I have more than a passing interest in personality, particularly in personal identity. The image which each one of us has of ourself is perhaps the single most important factor in helping us deal with day-to-day life. Each time a new situation is met, we tend to respond to it in ways which are consistent with our self-image. Because this process is so natural and permits us very quickly to evaluate most situations, it becomes an increasingly automatic process, and we come to rely heavily on knowing what to expect of ourselves. When, occasionally, we find ourselves doing things which do not fit with our self-image, we tend to say such things as: 'I don't understand it, that's not like me at all' or 'I'm just not myself lately.' It is an even more disturbing state of affairs when we find ourselves behaving in unexpected ways or feeling differently about something and then discover that somehow these unexpected reactions do fit with a changing self-image which we don't really know. It can be very frightening suddenly to discover that some fundamental change in us has left us not really knowing ourselves very well or what to expect of ourselves. It is this state of affairs to which the younger generation is often referring when they say, 'I need to get my head together.'

I have said all that I have about self-images so that we can better understand the cost involved when renewal reaches right into the very core of our being and begins to bring about changes not only in our life-style but in the very person we know or believe ourselves to be. If we look at Saul of Tarsus as he charges down the road to Damascus, we see a very self-confident young man. He knows who he is, what he's doing, where he's going, and why! Those followers of Jesus were dangerous; they were a threat to the old, established truth, and they had to be stopped. He, Saul, would gladly risk his own life, if necessary, to defend and preserve the old. He had already, as a matter of fact, watched over the garments of those who stoned Stephen. And now, he had applied for and received permission to bring back Christians as prisoners to Jerusalem, no doubt to meet the same fate as Stephen. Had we stopped this young Saul on his way to Damascus and asked him to tell us about himself, he would have had little trouble doing so: 'If any other man thinks he has reason for confidence in the flesh, I have more: circumcised on the eighth day, of the people of Israel, of the tribe of Benjamin, a Hebrew born of Hebrews; as to the law a Pharisee, as to zeal a persecutor of the church, as to righteousness under the law blameless' (Phil. 3: 4–6).

If now, however, we look in on the older Paul and ask him to tell us about himself, the picture would be far less precise, running all the way from dejection over his chains to pride in his apostleship: 'I am ". . . an apostle, (not of men, neither by man, but by Jesus Christ, and God the Father, who raised him from the dead)." Well no, not exactly, actually I am "the prisoner of the Lord . . . a servant of Jesus Christ . . . a servant unto all." But, ". . . I was not one whit behind the very chiefest apostle"; yet, on the other hand, "I am the least of the apostles, unfit to be called an apostle, because I persecuted the church of God" ' (Gal. 1: 1, Eph. 4: 1, Rom. 1: 1, 1 Cor. 9: 19, 2 Cor. 11: 5, AV, and 1 Cor. 15: 9). These are obviously the words of a Christian who has had to learn to know himself in moments of great honour and authority and in others of complete abasement and even embarrassment. In the first chapter alone of his second letter to Timothy, Paul uses the word 'ashamed' in three different instances in reference to his imprisonment. And, although he says that he himself is not ashamed, one doesn't have to be much of a psychologist to know the inner struggles that those references to shame suggest, especially in terms of his self-image and what others might think of one who makes claims of apostleship but has been a prisoner for so long.

If we consider the whole idea of certainty of purpose and direction, we find another obvious change from Saul to Paul. Saul knew exactly where he was going and why; he saw something that needed to be done, and he went straight forward into the task. But if we look at Paul's second missionary journey as our example, a very different picture emerges (Acts 15: 36–18: 22). He and Barnabas had decided to return to the cities where they had preached the Gospel on their first journey and to see to the welfare of the converts

74

they had made in those places. But, before they could get started, they argued over whether or not to take Mark with them. The argument was so sharp that they parted company, and Paul took Silas with him instead. In spite of the intended purpose of the journey (which had been Paul's idea), after the first four cities (at most) they never again touched the cities or churches of the first journey. As a matter of fact, they decided, at some point, to go into Asia; but the Spirit forbade them. Not knowing, then, exactly where to go, they remained in Phrygia and Galatia. Paul, apparently, only intended to pass through Galatia, but he became ill and had to remain there in order to recuperate. It was during that unintended stay that he founded the churches of Galatia – not by intent but by accident! (Gal. 4: 12–15). After he and the others left Galatia, they decided to go into Bithynia; but, again, the Spirit said, 'No!', so they went to Troas instead. It was there that Paul had the vision of the man from Macedonia saying, 'Come over to Macedonia and help us.' And immediately, in response to that call, they made straight for Philippi in Macedonia.

The story of Philippi is not one of great revival! Lydia, a merchant woman, was converted. A demon-possessed girl was delivered; and, for that, Paul and Silas were beaten and thrown in prison. That night the jailor and his family were converted and baptised, and the next day Paul and the others left town. While I certainly would not want to minimise the founding of the church at Philippi, the fact remains that it was not until their visit to Thessalonica that anything like great revival is evident. There is no doubt that Paul and Silas, as well as Timothy and Luke who had joined them during the journey, were fulfilling God's will. But it must be noted that, for a great deal of the time, all Paul really knew was where he was *not* supposed to go. As we follow Paul, we are not tracing footsteps of great insight or of Saul-like determination but the somewhat faltering steps of a dedicated man seeking to discover God's will in the midst of many uncertainties. I can't believe that Saul would have been a great admirer of this man, Paul! This Paul believed that God chooses 'what is foolish in the world to shame the wise . . . what is weak in this world to shame the strong' (1 Cor. 1: 27). Somehow that kind of thinking doesn't seem to fit Saul of Tarsus – or the John Wayne syndrome for that matter! It sounds more like a man who's been made a fool that he might be wise! How strange that Saul's personal renewal should take a self-assured, confident young man and make of him a fool for Christ's sake. How incredible that his transformation should cause him to glory in his infirmities in order to fit him to speak to a generation caught in unbelievable religious, social, and political upheaval, as well as to the Church for as long as it shall stand upon the earth!

Before leaving the subject of self-image or self-identity, let's consider Timothy (Acts 16: 1–3). His father was a Greek and his mother a Jew. Due, undoubtedly, to his father's prerogative, Timothy was not circumcised; therefore, lawfully, he was a Gentile. He was a convert to Christ (very possibly through Paul on his first missionary journey). When Paul and Silas passed through Lystra on the second journey, Paul wanted Timothy to accompany them for the remainder of the journey. But, there were many Jews in the places where Paul wanted to take Timothy as his companion. Therefore, Paul circumcised Timothy in order to make him acceptable to the Jews. Strangely enough, Paul had already refused to circumcise Titus to please the Jews at Jerusalem (Gal. 2: 3–5) and would soon write such statements as, '... neither circumcision counts for anything, nor uncircumcision, but a new creation' (Gal. 6:15). What is even more ironic is that when Timothy assumed a pastorate it was in Ephesus, a Gentile city well known for heathenism and idolatry where Timothy's assumed Jewishness through circumcision would have had little, if any, meaning.

A brief restatement of Timothy's personal history is most interesting: Born of mixed Greek and Jewish parentage, he was raised a Gentile, converted to Christianity, made acceptable to the Christian Jews through circumcision, and, by the same means, aliented from his Gentile heritage. By circumcision, he was made acceptable to minister amongst the Jewish Christians, but his pastorate was in a Gentile city and church! Certainly there doesn't seem to be any other New Testament believer with quite so varied a background. He must surely be one of those 'new creations' Paul wrote about. At first glance it would appear that he no longer really fitted or 'belonged' anywhere. But, at second glance, perhaps it's that he fitted and belonged everywhere! Renewal does that: Americans in Britain, Britons in Germany, Germans in Canada, Canadians in Israel, and so it goes in

76

this day of renewal. Thousands of Christians around the world are being renewed and reshaped to belong to the world-wide Body of Christ. God, by his Spirit, is fashioning those who can forget their past and their prejudices in order to 'belong' to whatever family of believers the Spirit ordains.

Having discussed the renewal in terms of changes in personal identity, we must also consider changes in terms of cultural norms and values. One set of ideals which pervades Western society has to do with ambition, training, and occupation. Very early in a child's life, we want him to begin to think about what he wants to be 'when he grows up'. One very practical reason for our concern that the decision come as early as possible is the long years of training which many modern technical fields require. What happens to those carefully laid plans when the Holy Spirit steps in to redirect lives in renewal?

Let's look again at Saul of Tarsus. He was a Hellenistic Jew and understood both the Greek and Aramaic languages. He had knowledge of both the Greek culture and philosophy. His formal education probably took place at either the university of Athens or of Tarus.[1] We do know that he was a pupil of Gamaliel, which no doubt accounts for his great knowledge of the Old Testament as well as his dedication as a Pharisee (Acts 22: 3). In addition to his formal education, he was trained as a tentmaker (Acts 18: 3). Although we in the Church have come to consider Paul as one of the single most important gifts of God to the Church, had we been members of his family or one of his tutors, our feelings very probably would have been quite different. What a waste of a life! His was a brilliant mind, remarkable training and education, and a promising future. And for what purpose? Rotting away in a Roman prison for following that crazy new religion – Christianity! The regard in which Saul was held by the religious leaders is evidenced by the authority they vested in him when they commissioned his venture in Damascus. I'm confident that there were tears shed in disappointment at the loss of one of such great promise. There can be no doubt that the Holy Spirit used Paul's mind and training as he ministered and, particularly, as he wrote the epistles, but these uses bear very little resemblance to the occupations for which his education and training were designed.

What about Luke the physician? How would it have felt to be a fully qualified doctor at a time in Church history when Peter's shadow would have had a higher recovery rate than one's practice? So much for training! I have a very real affinity for Luke in this regard. My own doctorate is in psychology. When I became a part of this renewal, I was the director of a student guidance centre; I had completed all the necessary course work for private practice; and I had already spent several years lecturing. And now, I'm back ministering in churches of all denominations – without even the security of a pulpit of my own – a task for which I was officially qualified before ever I returned to higher education. While I doubt that there have been any tears shed over the loss of me to academic or professional psychology, I'm sure there have been those who have shaken their heads in doubt, or even pity, at what seems an obvious waste of all those years of training and professional potential.

Finally, where training and occupation are concerned, what of the fishermen? The Scriptures tell us that Peter and Andrew left their nets but that James and John left both their nets *and* their father Zebedee. Zebedee and his wife were no doubt ambitious for their sons. It was, after all, James and John's mother who asked Jesus to allow her two sons to occupy the seats on either side of him when he came into his kingdom – no lack of ambition here! The theory seems to have been, if you're not going to make it to the top in the fish business, you should make it to the top of whatever you go into! There were two major points of renewal needed in that situation. One was to learn the new set of values which says, 'The last will be first, and the first last.' And the other was whatever transformation it is which turns fishermen into apostles!

Another set of ideals in our culture has to do with traditions, values, and customs. Among these values is our admiration for a well planned, ordered life. We admire the person who knows where he's going, who sets out in life with firm goals in mind, and who proceeds steadily toward their accomplishment. If I might be permitted one Old Testament example out of a 'renewal' of a different order, I'd like us to consider Abraham. We know from the scriptural record that he was seventy-five years old when God told him to leave his father's house and his kindred and nation. God gave him the promise that he would make him a great nation and, as we are told in the eleventh chapter of Hebrews, sent him to look for a city 'which has foundations, whose builder and maker is God'. But we also know that 'he went out, not knowing where he was to go'. Furthermore, we know that he dwelt in tents as a stranger in the land of promise and that he died in faith not having received what was promised, 'having seen it and greeted it from afar'. A vision of a city while you're still living in tents is not much of a substitute for the city itself, as our culture counts accomplishments. To the natural ear, such an explanation sounds like defensive illusions used to cover the foolish failures of a man who set out but never arrived at his dream. I wonder how many of us in this renewal will be able to hold faithful in the face of such apparent failure? The Church of the Lord Jesus Christ built of loving relationships between individuals who are open and honest with one another, living in unselfish interdependence – what a city to look for!

Another one of our ideals regarding traditions, values, and customs is our pride in family tradition. When James and John left their father Zebedee, did they consider who would assume the family business when he died? We know that, in the end, neither James nor John returned to their nets, and we really don't know what happened to the business. And yet, I imagine we do. More than likely, it was one of the 'costs of renewal'. I recall a day at Whittier College when a student who was one of the Jesus People came to see me in my office. His father was in his mid-forties and in very poor health due, according to the doctors, to over work and improper concern for his body – the typical overworked-executive syndrome. The young man had come to talk to me as a Christian lecturer. It seemed that the Lord was speaking to him about his future and what the Lord wanted of him, but his father already had plans for him which he had cherished since the boy's birth. It seemed that he was either to be a doctor or enter the father's business; these were the dreams for which the father had worked without regard for his own health. The question was: How to follow the Lord and the dictates of his own heart *and* to honour his father according to the Scriptures? He said to me, 'How do I tell my father that I don't want to arrive at forty-five with a big house and two cars and be broken in body in order to fulfil his dreams for me?' It was evident, of course, that the generation gap and a renewed young heart were all rolled into one problem. I wish I could tell you that I gave him a wise answer which solved the problem. What we did was to talk and pray together, and I felt the strange tug-of-war of one who could identify with both parties caught on either side of the renewal. Indeed, forsaking father and mother may not be an exaggeration as one counts the cost of renewal.

Finally, we need to consider the cost of doctrinal changes in renewal. The woman of Samaria ran into the village saying to the men, 'Come, see a man who told me all that I ever did. Can this be the Christ?' (John 4: 29). And yet, if we look at the whole episode, we find that Jesus had asked her about her husbands very early in the discussion. It may be true that it was the fact that he knew all that she had ever done which convinced her that he might well be the Christ, but that conclusion wasn't accepted until at least one doctrinal issue had been bandied about. She wanted Jesus to declare himself on the issue of whether Jerusalem or Samaria was the 'proper' place of worship. His answer was: 'Woman, believe me, the hour is coming when neither on this mountain nor in Jerusalem will you worship the Father ... the hour is coming, and now is, when the true worshippers will worship the Father in spirit and truth, for such the Father seeks to worship him' (John 4: 21-3). Christ's statement may have been the correct answer to her question, but it didn't settle the historical issue between the Jews and the Samaritans. I wonder what the modern-day equivalents to that question and that answer sound like!

When Nicodemus came to Jesus by night, it was because his doctrinal image of the Messiah and the person of Jesus and the miraculous works of Jesus simply did not fit together. If you follow their discussion (John 3: 1-21), you will see that Nicodemus interrupted twice as Jesus explained the mystery of the new birth. Each time it was to ask the question: 'How can this be?' Past doctrine simply did not fit with what Jesus was saying. We don't really know the end of Nicodemus' story. We have very little further mention of him in the Scriptures, but we do know one further bit about him. When all the disciples had fled, it was Nicodemus who claimed the body of Jesus. One wonders if he ever got his doctrine sorted out, or was it something else which compelled him to claim the Lord's body – something which overrides doctrine?

Doctrinal issues continue to plague the Church, and the style of this renewal is such that it isn't doing much to straighten them out. Somehow, the Holy Spirit seems to attach far less importance to doctrine than do most theologians and preachers – and many laymen as well. If you would like an exercise in a modern-day doctrinal debate, consider this: Imagine that it is your task to explain a 'charismatic, Spirit-filled, Roman Catholic priest' to Martin Luther! Renewal is so indifferent to the past. The Jews had suffered all manner of ridicule for their circumcision. How dare Paul say it availed nothing! They had paid a great price for their uniqueness. Some of our forefathers died to bring us religious liberties and the Scriptures in our own language; how dare anyone treat that lightly! Know this – either we bury the past, or it will bury us. This is a day of renewal. God is pouring out his Spirit upon all flesh; and, in this new day, old barriers are not only obsolete but an affront to the Spirit of God.

These are only some of the areas and issues involved in personal renewal. Who can say what shapes the new will take! At such a time, it is good to make as honest an appraisal of ourselves as possible. Even if we assent to renewal with our minds and mouths, our hearts often take longer to agree. For years many of us have sung the old hymn which says:

> Have thine own way Lord, have thine own way,
> Thou art the potter, I am the clay.

Those words contain a lovely sentiment, except that it's the wrong analogy for renewal. He may well be the potter, but we are anything but a lump of fresh, soft, pliable clay in the master's hand. Most of us are well set, well baked, hard, brittle, and even broken pots. When such as these are set on the wheel again, one hears the most anguished squeals and squawking, and one wonders if anything truly renewed could possibly come from such stuff! And yet, thank God, by his Spirit renewal is happening, and lives are being wonderfully and even miraculously transformed.

I've tried to help us be as forthright and honest as possible as we've discussed the cost of personal renewal. But, if (after all that we've talked about) you have counted the cost and you still want to be a part of what God is doing by his Spirit in this day of renewal in the Church, then come along and join the rest of us who have no idea what all the Lord is doing or what the end will be. We have only the same clue as Abraham: We look 'forward to the city which has foundations, whose builder and maker is God'.

As we have noted, this renewal is particularly involved with love and loving relationships within the Body of Christ. The renewed individual does not need to struggle on his own with the cost of his personal renewal, with his fears of love, or with past hurts. It is not intended that he should be separated from other Christians unto God. He is to be set within the framework of the Body – in loving, committed relationships. In order for all this to be so, the Holy Spirit must be able to renew not only individuals but whole fellowships. Thank God, this is happening. Within these renewed fellowships, one often sees a pattern something like this: The individual believer is brought into a loving encounter with another believer (or believers), and the Holy Spirit uses that loving encounter to heal and restore that which past hurt or fear of love or fear of change has damaged. Then, when such initial healing and restoring have taken place, the individual is able to be even more open and honest and to enter more deeply into loving relationships. Such deepening relationships are then instrumental in even further healing and wholeness. I must be honest and say, however, that this on-going process itself involves the risk of hurt, since neither we nor those we love and who love us are perfect in that love. Therefore, let us now consider the whole area of fullness of life and the processes of healing through loving relationships within the Body of Christ.

7. Loving Relationships within the Body of Christ

There is the very real sense in which all true believers in Christ throughout the world and throughout all the ages comprise the Body of Christ. But, there is also just as real a sense in which the members of each local fellowship of believers are the Body of Christ, the Church, in a particular time and place. Certainly the epistles to the churches were addressed to local bodies of believers, and the instructions contained in them were intended to be lived out in local fellowships. In the simplest terms, then, a group of individual believers in loving, committed relationships with one another are the Body of Christ.

While it has been necessary for us to consider the cost of renewal in terms of change for the individual, in fact, the very nature of the current renewal requires that we become increasingly less individualistic and more involved in loving one another. It cannot be denied that some aspects of Christianity can be accomplished individually. For example, we may become more aware of lost souls around the world or feel a deepening compassion for the poor and underprivileged on our own. But, if we are going to open our lives to one another, to love and to be loved in interdependent relationships as this renewal requires, we simply will not be able to remain independent of one another. Therefore, we must come to understand the renewal in terms of the quality of our relationships within the Body, if we are going to appreciate fully the implications of the renewal for ourselves, the Church, and the world at large. Furthermore, the fact that the true measure of the particular facet of the renewal which we are discussing is the quality of loving relationships means that we must see entire local congregations renewed in their love for one another. Such a renewal of love and care within the body will provide the proper framework and atmosphere for the growth and development of the loving relationships in which the individual may, in turn, develop.

In chapter five, we considered some of the changes in attitudes and behaviour which are coming within the Church. But, if we are going to understand how these changes fit into the whole pattern of renewal, we must have a renewed vision of just what life in the Body of Christ is intended to be. Such a vision will challenge many of the ways in which we have allowed the life-style within our churches to be conformed to social structures and attitudes in the society at large. But, if we can catch such a vision and experience such a renewal, then the Church will once again stand out in bold relief to offer a real alternative to a way of life which has brought so much loneliness and fear.

Literally hundreds of books have been written on the subject of the formal structure of the Church in terms of authority, government, and ministries. I would like us, rather, to consider something far less formal, something not centred around any structure of roles. I would like us to consider the quality of life which we are intended to share within the family of believers in order that each of us may be fulfilled in the nature with which God has created us and in order that our shared life might speak to the world about Jesus. To do so, let me start by restating just a few of the facts about man with which we dealt in chapter two. One of the most fundamental facts which we discussed about man is that, as a creature created in the image of God, he should not be alone (Gen. 2: 18). Further, we noted that two are better than one because they are available to one another for help and reassurance (Eccles. 4: 9–12). These factors underlie all of God's planning for man. Thus, mutually beneficial roles of interdependence mark every social structure which God has designed. For example, consider the family: father, mother, husband, wife, son, daughter, parent, child, brother, sister, etc. Each of these roles is defined in terms of its relationship to the others. In no instance is one role simply to benefit another; they are always reciprocal roles of mutual love, support, and responsibility. Even a structure as large as the nation Israel was based upon enlarged family units in which individuals helped and cared for one another. Christ's definition of so casual a relationship as neighbour is that of one who actively gives himself to another. And most especially the Church is an interdependent body. The very analogy of the *body* points out how impossible it is for the Church to function unless each

84

part is working properly (Eph. 4: 15–16) and unless the unity is such that 'if one member suffers, all suffer together; if one member is honoured, all rejoice together' (1 Cor. 12: 26).

But the Church is much more than a social structure based upon mutual help and support amongst its members. It is the very Body of Christ – the residing place of all true believers and the Holy Spirit which inhabits and empowers it. The Church is the family of God; as such, the relationships within it are definable in terms of that which one member provides for another and is provided for in return. Jesus said that they who do the will of God are his mother, his sister, or his brother (Mark 3: 35). The Father himself is a father to the fatherless (Ps. 68: 5). These statements refer to more than spiritualised truths. The Body of Christ gives these promises substance. Loving relationships within the Church are God's tangible provision for his children for whom it is not good to be alone. Our tendency to 'spiritualise' much of the scriptural record has caused us to miss many of the far simpler and more basic truths about love. The fact is that we have been made members of Christ and of one another. As such, we are intended to love one another with tenderness and feeling as members of the same family. The bonds which such love ensures are intended to provide the care and support which each of us need to survive and to develop the God-given potentials within us.

The informal structure which emerges, then, is as follows: there are the individual members of the body who are the individual believers. But a body is not a collection of identical and individual parts; thus, individual members are grouped to form segments or organs of the body. These are the particular relationships (and even small groups of relationships) in which the Lord involves the individual members (Eph. 4: 15–16). This pattern of loving relationships in which individuals work out their callings and ministries, as well as being sustained and built up, is consistently found in the New Testament. Pairs and small groups of believers are so consistent a pattern in the early church that, in fact, one finds only the rarest instances of individuals living, travelling, or working on their own. But, beyond that, these relationships and small groupings are fitted into the larger whole of the local body and, finally, into the Universal Body of Christ. The dynamic, then, is that the individual member is sustained by the relationships which are his, and those relationships themselves are supported and sustained by the larger body. Thus, as the individual faces problems, or even a breaking point, loving, sustaining relationships are there to support and heal. And, when there is breakdown in such relationships themselves, the larger body is there to support, sustain, and heal.

The picture of the Church as a body made up of individuals in loving, committed relationships, rather than independent individuals related only to Christ who are held together by a common set of beliefs, does require some changes in our approach to church life and function. For one thing, it means that pastoral care and teaching within the local body must take relationship dynamics into consideration. Individuals cannot be counselled, ministered to, or cared for independent of those with whom they share their lives. It means, too, that shared ministries, as well as shared lives, must be recognised. When Paul came to minister, the local church got not only Paul but Luke and Timothy and others as well, because such a shared ministry was more profitable than Paul ever could have been on his own. The value which we are to one another in all facets of our lives and ministries within the Church simply must be recognised and provided for if the Church is to be renewed and individual believers made whole. To whatever extent shared lives and shared ministries require the local church (or whole denominations and movements) to reorder its priorities or re-allocate its existing time, energy, or funds, we can expect the Holy Spirit to so direct and teach us. On the other hand, to whatever extent *additional* time, effort, or income is required, we can expect God to sustain or provide as necessary. It is both faulty logic and false economy which attempts to conserve the Lord's resources by reducing the quality of life or ministry within the Body of Christ. Shared lives and shared ministries require that we be prepared to 'spend' the resources of the body in new, or renewed, ways. That we can find cheaper, faster, or even easier ways to do the thing may well be true; but, if such 'savings' destroy or even reduce abundant life, they are not savings – they are robbery!

The idea that loving relationships within the Body are necessary and appropriate and that such relationships themselves need support and care is not, in fact, a new idea within the Church or limited to this renewal. Matthew Henry, who

86

died in 1714, included such an idea when he wrote concerning Paul and Barnabas and their quarrel. He notes that Paul, when he desires to go again to minister, turns 'to Barnabas, his old friend and fellow-labourer; he invites his company and help in this work. We have need one of another, and may be in many ways serviceable one to another; and therefore should be forward both to borrow and lend assistance. Two are better than one. Every soldier has his comrade.' And, then, in discussing the quarrel which separated them before the journey could be undertaken, Matthew Henry says, 'And they were certainly both in fault to be hot as to let the contention be sharp (it is to be feared they gave one another some hards words), as also to be so stiff as to stick resolutely to his opinion, and neither to yield. It is a pity that they did not refer the matter to a third person, or that some friend did not interpose to prevent its coming to an open rupture. Is there never a wise man among them to interpose his good offices, and to accommodate the matter ...?'[1] The idea that every soldier has his comrade is well attested to throughout Church history. On a plaque of dedication in the Fletcher Memorial Methodist Church in Madeley, Telford, Shropshire, are these words by John Wesley concerning his friend and co-labourer, John Fletcher: '... A helpmeet to me in every respect, where could I have found another such?'

True love is the most fundamental bond within the family of God. Every other function within the Body of Christ takes its impetus from love. Paul declares: 'Put on then, as God's chosen ones, holy and beloved, compassion, kindness, lowliness, meekness, and patience, forbearing one another and, if one has a complaint against another, forgiving each other; as the Lord has forgiven you, so you also must forgive. And above all these put on love, which binds everything together in perfect harmony' (Col. 3: 12–14). Out of such love and harmony comes a willingness to share ourselves, our very souls, not just our Gospel (1 Thess. 2: 8). That idea is often especially difficult for many Evangelicals who pride themselves that their only link and relationship with one another is Jesus himself. I will grant that the only basis for family relationships within the Body of Christ is Jesus, but that is simply to say that we are new creatures in Christ who have been called to love one another with a love which includes both *agape* and *phileo*. In that love, we give

87

ourselves to one another as Jesus gave himself to us in truth and love.

There can be no doubt that Jesus and his disciples dearly loved one another. Christ called them to follow him and to becomes fishers of men and proclaimers of the kingdom. But his relationship with them was not in any way limited to that of teacher or co-worker. He called them his friends (John 15: 15). He used his love for them as the proper measure of their love for each other (John 13: 34). John rested his head upon Jesus' breast, and he referred to himself as the 'disciple whom Jesus loved'. In chapter three, we discussed Jesus' questions to Peter regarding Peter's love for him. Their discussion took place after Peter had denied Jesus and had gone back to his boat and nets. It is very interesting to note that Jesus' concern was not, 'Peter do you believe what I say now?' or 'Peter will you be more faithful in the future?' but 'Peter do you love me?' The assurance of Peter's love was the important issue for Jesus; it was the single thing in that moment that really mattered to him.

True love, which combines both *agape* and *phileo*, builds enduring relationships. Such bonds amongst the first-century Christians were so strong that they relied upon *family* terms to indicate and describe them. Paul writes to Timothy, 'his dearly beloved son', and to Titus, 'his true child'. But more than these endearing terms is the tenderness and concern which marks these relationships. Paul writes to Timothy, his beloved son, and begs him to come to him in prison so that Timothy might be near him during the last days of his life. Paul says to him, 'Get Mark and bring him with you . . . do your best to come before winter . . . I remember your tears . . . I long night and day to see you, that I may be filled with joy' (2 Tim. 4: 11).

The aged John writes to 'his beloved children' and repeatedly refers to them as his beloved. He speaks of his desire to see those he loves and says that his joy will not be complete until he sees them face to face rather than writing to them with paper and ink (2 John 12). The very fact that affectionate letters, such as these by Paul and John, were written amongst believers indicates the strength and permanence of their love for one another. These are not friendships between people who go to the same church! These are loving relationships between members of the same family. These members of the family love each other dearly and have unashamedly committed to one another the same affection and faithfulness which they have committed to Christ himself.

In discussing incidents of loving, committed relationships in the Scriptures, I would like to briefly refer again to David and Jonathan. Their love for each other stands as an example of so much that is true love. Their affection for one another is undoubtable. They wept at parting; and, when apart, they longed for one another. They pledged themselves each to the other and were faithful throughout the whole of their lives to their vow. As a matter of fact, David continued to honour his vow even to Jonathan's son long after Jonathan was dead. David declared that Jonathan's love was better to him than the love of women. David was a mighty man of valour and a fierce soldier, but he loved Jonathan tenderly and faithfully as one who belonged to him.

With such perfect examples of love in the relationships between God's children, how could modern Christianity have been so blind to the place of such love in our relationships? How could we have failed to encourage men to love one another deeply? How could we have come to believe that the only truly committed relationships are within marriage or blood family? How could we have encouraged every individual to stand on his own two feet without the stabilising benefit of emotional ties within the family of God? God forgive us for our foolishness!

Thankfully, he not only forgives us, but he's restoring us. The current renewal in the Church is in many ways a return to loving, dependable, committed relationships – a return to spiritual family. This is family not by natural birth or legal bonds but family constituted in the Body of Christ and bonded by love. It is not surprising then to discover that all over the world a new, or renewed, degree of love is marking the relationships amongst believers. A new sense of belonging, of honesty, of care, and of family is developing within the renewed Church. The result is that the word is once again beginning to see something tangible and real within the Church, something they can believe.

It was this very factor of 'outsiders' becoming family which gave Deb and me our first real adjustment problem as we became more involved in the Church renewal. Deb simply could not understand what was happening to me. I had always been very reserved and proper with people outside

89

our family. I think it would be honest to say that many people would have considered me aloof – an air which is most often a cover-up for fear but is one which the traditional role of 'pastor' encourages. Furthermore, an additional factor marked the relationship between Deb and me. When we married, my children were in their early teens, and I had taken care to ensure Deb's place at my side and in our home as wife and mother. This carefulness meant that Deb had always known a really guarded place in my life and my love. The combination of my reserve and my carefulness for Deb meant that she had only ever seen me show affection to the other members of our close family. Then, suddenly, the Lord began to put others into my life who seemed like family to me. I simply loved them, and I didn't know why or what it meant or what was happening to me.

The first such experience happened the last night of those first youth camps at Post Green. We had had a wonderful service which concluded outdoors around a large bonfire. After the meeting was officially over, the young people stayed around the fire singing and chatting. Everyone seemed reluctant to leave. At some point, Deb and I began to go round the fire and to say good-bye to as many of the young people as we could. Amongst the campers was a young lad about seventeen years old named David. His parents were a part of the Post Green staff. Although he had been to both weeks of camp, he hadn't really been involved; actually, he was rather shy and withdrawn. As I was saying good-bye to others, I came up to David standing by the fire, and I put my arm around his shoulder to say a rather 'proper' good-bye – after all, we'd barely spoken to one another before this time. But, as I put my arm around his shoulder, he turned half-way round, laid his head on my chest, and began to weep softly.

You must remember that I was still pretty new at this sort of thing. My first response was that of a minister. I waited an *appropriate* few minutes and then said, 'David, can I pray with you about anything?' He said, 'No.' So, I waited another *appropriate* few minutes and responded as a psychologist. I said, 'David, can I talk to you about anything?' He said, 'No.' By this time, I was out of professional roles. So, I waited a *not-quite-so-appropriate* few minutes and said, 'Is there anything I can do for you?', to which he replied, 'No.' Degrees, training, and years of experience notwithstanding, I can be rather dense sometimes! It simply didn't occur to me that – while I was standing there with my arms around him trying to figure out the right thing to do – I was doing it! In situations like that, preachers pray and psychologists talk, but what do people do? What does one do to fill the awkward silences? We get so accustomed to our roles dictating the right responses for us to make in social situations. Besides which, 'just being there' is such a hard thing to do! It doesn't follow any of the technical rules of social or professional performance. How does anyone ever qualify for a certificate in 'just being there'?

After a rather long time, I decided that perhaps one of the reasons he didn't move away from me was that he simply didn't know quite how to break away graciously. After all, people do get themselves into situations which they then find difficult to get out of. Perhaps he was just a little embarrassed. (You don't have to be much of a psychologist to figure out who was most embarrassed.) At any rate, I decided to shift my position a little to give him an opportunity to move away toward some of the other young people, if he wished. So, I moved my stance just slightly, and he moved to accommodate! Each time I moved, so did he. Finally, after a very long time, I said, 'David, I'm going in to bed now, can I walk you to your tent?' And he said, 'No.' There didn't seem to be anything else to do – so I went to bed.

The thing that was so amazing, however, was what happened when I saw David the next day. I had such an overwhelming love for him. It was unlike any experience I'd ever known outside my family, and I certainly had no idea, at the time, what it meant. Deb and I remained in England for nine weeks that first summer; and, toward the end of our stay, we had an opportunity to spend another week with some of the staff at Post Green. During that week, David spent a great deal of time with us. I came to love him even more; and he, obviously, loved me as well. It should be noted that David is from a fine family and has two brothers. In none of the stereotyped ways was I necessary to him as a substitute for 'real family' which was missing. The Lord simply gave us to one another as family. I think it is probably important for me to say here that neither Deb nor I had heard, at that time, that such loving, family relationships were happening anywhere else to anyone else. It seemed a strange, rather isolated experience.

For Deb, David posed a real problem. We had come to England on a working holiday with plenty of spare time allotted for us to be on our own to do all of the things we enjoyed. Now, suddenly, there was someone else who wanted to be around and to be included in what we were doing. Furthermore, I wanted him around, too, but Deb didn't really feel any of the love which I had for him. I recall one situation which seems rather amusing now, but it wasn't at the time. We were going to go for a drive, and David and I went out to the car ahead of Deb. David got into the front seat next to me. It may seem a little thing, but that place had always belonged to Deb, and I had always protected it for her as a part of her role in our family. But, somehow, in such a situation, it didn't occur to me to fall back on established patterns and roles, and David stayed in the front seat. For Deb, it was just one more indication that things were happening to us which were going to make life very different from now on, and she wasn't at all sure, at that point, that she wanted life to be all that different!

There really isn't space to recount all the ways in which David became dear to me and, finally, to both of us. But today, after nearly four years of living in England, David is a very real part of our life and family. He simply belongs to us and we to him – with all the joys and responsibility of family. Actually, David has been just one part of the Lord working to open both Deb and me and our marriage to include others. Even stable marriages need renewing in this day of renewal!

It was much later, however, that we began to discover that what was happening to Deb and me was happening in various ways all over the world. It was only after we began to realise that the Lord was developing his Body into real family again that our experiences in love began to make sense in a larger context. During the years which have passed since that first summer, the Lord has brought several people into our lives and even into our home. These are not people to whom we have 'ministered' in any formal sense, any more than any family would use the term *ministry* for the love and care they provide for one another. We simply love each other, share life together, and the Lord uses us to develop and open one another in true spiritual growth.[2]

Family love, such as we've been discussing, demands a certain quality of relating. Family relationships are marked by patience and love, and they require a great deal of giving to and taking from one another. Such giving and taking go beyond the usual, agreed-upon patterns of social interaction – especially since the people involved do not fall into our usual definition of family. Such relating requires, therefore, not only a change in our definition of family but in our attitudes about giving and receiving. In chapter six, we talked about the cost of renewal in terms of personal change. Now, we need to discuss challenges to several of our shared values – those agreed-upon ideals which govern our social interaction – what, how, and when do I give and do I receive?

8. The Cost of Loving Relationships is Even More Change

In Paul's first letter to the Corinthians, we are told that God has designed the Body of Christ such that the members are to have 'the same care for one another' (1 Cor. 12: 25). The picture is that of a body in which the welfare of each member is the concern of the other members. The care described is mutual, interdependent, loving care. No member is to be exempt from such care, nor is any member expected to function without it. In the simplest terms such mutual care means that each member will be both a giver and a receiver regularly, consistently, and often simultaneously. But, for us in Western culture, it's not that simple. We have very real problems both when we give and when we receive. These problems come from our agreed-upon, cultural attitudes about giving and receiving. But, if deep, loving relationships can only be built within the Body of Christ by both giving to and receiving from one another, then the cost of such relationships is even more change! In this case, the change must come in the way we think about giving and receiving so that we can be free truly to function together as Christ's Body.

Let us consider first some of the problems we face when we are the giver. The most obvious problem, of course, is that of motive. Jesus warns us to be sure when we give not to do so in order to be seen of men (Matt. 6: 1–4 and 23: 1–2). Christ's warning deals primarily with the fact that such giving loses its eternal reward, since God judges the motive not the deed. Paul speaks to the same issue: '. . . If I give away all I have . . . but have not love, I gain nothing' (1 Cor. 13: 3). Paul is here speaking of the loss which occurs when an apparently loving deed is done without love. Again, God judges motive. But reward is not the only loss which occurs when deeds are done to satisfy appearance rather than from the heart; there is also a real loss in quality. Such losses become very apparent if we compare the quality of deeds which are done out of love with the quality of those same deeds done out of duty.

Throughout the years that our two children were growing up, we had a rule in our home that they each were to keep their own room clean and tidy. As they grew older, that rule became increasingly difficult to enforce. But, every so often, Dad would reach a certain limit and declare 'National Room Cleaning Day'. On such a day, there was usually a further announcement that no friends were to come to visit; there were to be no prolonged phone conversations; and, in fact, there was to be as little contact as possible with the outside world – until those rooms were clean! Those were often painful days. I would get called in to inspect first one room and then the other at about three-minute intervals, each time in the hope that I would say that the room was clean enough. After each non-successful inspection, there would be a flurry of drawers and doors slamming, a few odd bangs, and then another call for inspection. Actually, I'm not talking about demands that the rooms be in perfect order; I'm talking about rooms with a sufficiently clear thoroughfare so that one could successfully move from one side to the other without endangering life or limb! Usually, I decided that the rooms were clean enough when the inspection tours finally wore me out, and we would call a truce until the next time.

But there were other days. Every so often I would be awakened on a Saturday morning by the hum of the Hoover. As I would go down the hall to see what was going on, a voice would call out, 'Don't come in yet, I want to surprise you.' Two or three golden hours would sometimes pass; and, finally, when I was invited in to see, the room would fairly dazzle. I suppose that, technically, after either procedure one could say, 'The children cleaned their rooms today.' But the events being described would be vastly different, as would be the quality of the final product. What a difference between the performance of love and duty!

Somehow, the Church – with its lack of warm, tender love – has become very duty oriented. Therefore, as the Holy Spirit is seeking to make us a loving family once more, his prime objective for us is love which will motivate the very laying down of our lives for one another. We simply cannot be to one another what God intends us to be out of a sense of duty or requirement. It is vital that we stop believing that duty will do where love is required.

Strangely enough, as important as motive is, it is often our very concern over motive which leads some of us into another problem where giving is concerned. The problem has to do with an attitude of false 'selflessness'. Because the Scriptures warn us about self-serving motives, we often conclude that there must be no self-fulfilment at all! But here, we need balance. If we don't feel a real joy in that which we do for others, we won't do it for long, certainly no longer than duty demands! Don't forget that 'the joy of the Lord is your strength' (Neh. 8: 10). Even Christ endured the cross because of the 'joy that was set before him' (Heb. 12: 2). Where love is concerned, we are told to love our neighbour as ourself – not instead of ourself. The scriptural warning about motive has to do with deeds done to be seen of men or pretending to be what we are not. There is no warning against being fulfilled and joyous in the things we do for one another because it feels so good to love and to be loved. Christ does not want us to put on false fronts in order to make a good impression, but he does want us to be deeply fulfilled in our love for one another. We must learn, therefore, to allow ourselves to enjoy and to take warmth from those things which we do for those we love.

Another problem attitude, which is very prevalent in our culture, centres around our concern for skills. We have become a highly trained, skilled people. We are offered education and training in nearly every subject under the sun. Therefore, when we require services of any sort, we tend to consult the expert in the particular field in question. Along with such an emphasis on expertise, has come a genuine mistrust of anything which does not come out of formal preparation. It is not surprising, then, to find this same attitude expressed in the Church. Even within the renewal movement, classes, books, seminars, and courses of the 'how-to' variety abound. The real problem arises when we offer one another only our skill, training, or expertise and fail to include ourselves, 'our very souls'. Even the ministries and gifts within the Body can be dispensed with an air of professionalism which destroys even the semblance of family and shared life. The things we can *do* for one another are important but not as important as what we *are* to one another.

Another cultural norm which we have adopted in the Church is very much related to professionalism. It is the value which holds that a cool, objective, detached performance of any function is to be preferred to one which is warm, involved, or sentimental. But Jesus was not cool and detached when he cleansed the temple or sought Peter again from his boat. These issues and people mattered deeply to him, and he was involved with all his heart. That is why it finally broke. Hearts only break when they're crushed by things which truly matter.

Some time ago, Deb and I were invited to a large charismatic church in England. Amongst other things, the church had a good-sized staff of counsellors whose task it was to be available to people for prayer and counsel. They were identified by badges and were, by and large, the leading members of the congregation. As a Christian psychologist, I was invited to a one-day conference to teach and give further training to these counsellors. During the course of the morning, I talked about the need to give ourselves rather than our skills, or even our 'ministries'; and, then, we opened the meeting for discussion. Almost immediately one of the senior counsellors challenged me and said, 'I'm not so sure about this whole counselling business. I sometimes think that people don't want answers to their problems at all. When you give them the scriptural answer to one problem, they just come up with another one. I think they just want to take up your time.' And with that, I was supposed to respond.

All I could say to him was, 'You're right; they don't simply want answers; they want you.' What had happened was this: The church, in its effort to be helpful, had set up a system in which counsellors were available to anyone with a problem. In such systems, however, the only legitimate reason for taking up the time of a counsellor is a problem. Furthermore, these counsellors had become so skilled at scriptural answers that a normal, run-of-the-mill problem would only 'purchase a few minutes of friendship'. The only alternative, if you wanted more time, was to come up with another problem fast! Most people don't really want counsel and advice, as such; they crave love. They really don't need the services of a 'dedicated servant of the Lord'; they need a Christian brother or sister who will weep when they weep and rejoice when they rejoice and who will love them and be loved by them. How strange that, at a time when the secular world is beginning to question the validity of social roles and professionalised relations,[1] so many in the Church should still cling to such ideals for relationships in the Body of Christ.

I feel that it is vital to pursue this point further, since we often feel that the degree of professionalism or detachment which is required in any particular case is determined by the seriousness of the problem. While Deb and I were at Post Green, we came to know a young woman named Sony who was a student at Christian Life College (which, at that time, was associated with Post Green). Sony's childhood had been tragic, but she had married a Christian young man, and they had had a son who was, by this time, about two years old. By all outward appearances, Sony and Alastair's life was rather typical of many Christian young couples who are starting out to build a new family. However, little by little, Sony had begun to experience bouts of depression which had become increasingly frequent and severe. By the time I met Sony, she was frequently completely immobilised by depression, fears, and confusion. Very often, nothing in her world gave life any real meaning. I recall one day when she came into our living room and, with tears streaming down her face, said, 'Why do you have to go on living when you don't want to? It's not fair; you ought to be able to stop when it hurts too much to go on.' There were no verbal answers I could give; all I could do was hold her and let her know I loved her.

And I did love Sony. I felt that the Lord had given me a love for her almost immediately when we met. Actually, there were four or five of us in the community who especially loved Sony. Often she did nothing more than come to one of us and cry in our arms for five minutes and then go away again. Sometimes, she would come and stay with Deb and me for several hours. One of those who was especially close to Sony was Pinky Ball, the wife of one of the teachers in the community. At one stage, Pinky encouraged Sony to attempt to write out her feelings if she could. The result is some of the simplest and most beautiful poetry I know. The following poem is one which Sony wrote in the depths of her depression:

Time passes slowly in my wood.

There are no flowers or sunshine in this dark deserted
place.
I am alone, so very much alone.
How desperately I want to leave this dreadful wood.
Sometimes I meet creatures who love on my way,
But rarely do I recognise this love.
The darkness is so intense.
I want to walk out into the sunshine,
But I don't believe it is there any more.
I keep bumping into trees and falling down.
Each time I fall, the longer it takes me to get up again.
The wood is a very familiar place now,
But the hate I have for it comes from deep within me.
And yet there are times when I find it almost bearable.
Must I go on living here?
Oh unknown path to me, that could my freedom be,
I am a stranger in this place; may it never be my home:
The endless searching for a way out,
The unhappiness it causes me, each time leading into
more darkness.
My feet are incapable of leading me home;
They cannot understand the directions.
God, please don't let me die here—
Please let me see the sun again.[2]

I wish I could tell you that healing for Sony came quickly
or easily, but that's not true. A childhood filled with hurt
and loneliness seldom mends overnight. But it does mend.
Today, Sony is a happy and incredibly insightful wife and
mother. I visited her and Alastair in their home recently,
and she said to me, 'I see so much hurt in people I meet, and
most of them aren't getting any real help – not even in their
churches. Somehow, I seem to know how they feel.' Sony
stands out in my mind and life because hers is not a success
story of therapeutic technique or of a proper method of
counselling but, rather, of love that was as constantly available as those of us who particularly loved Sony could collectively make it. Sony certainly didn't get much in the way
of 'professional' help from me, but she did get, and still has,
a little part of my life and heart.

Before we talk about attitudes associated with receiving,
let's discuss one more problem associated with giving. It is
the attitude which we have about the worthiness of the

receiver. Somehow, before we give our time or our concern, we want to know that the other person is in some way worth our effort; we want to see some evidence of worthiness. We also want to see that the person is serious and not just 'wasting our time'. On that basis, Zacchaeus was a poor risk! Certainly the crowd let Jesus know what they thought of him. The only motive which the Scriptures give for his climbing the tree was curiosity. In addition, we know that he was rich, a traitor to Israel, and undoubtedly unscrupulous. And Jesus chose his home for his abode, and that simple, loving gesture transformed Zacchaeus' life (Luke 19: 1–10).

We are warned in the Scriptures about our prejudices where others are concerned. James tells us that choosing between men because of their wealth or status is sin (Jas. 2: 1–7). The writer to the Hebrews warns that we may miss a blessing: 'Do not neglect to show hospitality to strangers, for thereby some have entertained angels unawares' (Heb. 13: 2). It is absolutely vital that we get over our prejudices in this day of renewal. Whether they are based on race, nationality, sex, education, appearance, common interests, doctrinal agreement, or any other factor, they destroy the unity of the family; and they rob us of our love for one another. It's a heartwarming thing to see men and women from all walks of life and from all backgrounds truly loving one another. Paul states, 'There is neither Jew nor Greek, there is neither slave nor free, there is neither male nor female; for you are all one in Christ Jesus' (Gal. 3: 28). Therefore, we deny our calling in Christ and defraud the world of its God-given right to see our love for one another if we place any prerequisite on our willingness to love.

Now, let's discuss some of our attitudes associated with being the receiver in social situations and particularly how such attitudes impair mutually caring relationships. First, let us consider the general attitude which holds that the one who receives is in some way weaker than the one who gives. Such an idea leads to all sorts of 'games playing'. For one thing, we often find it necessary to interpret a give-and-take situation in terms of our *wanting* help rather than *needing* it; or we construe the situation such that it appears that we need help only because there isn't enough time for us to do all that we've so generously taken on. In such situations, we can allow ourselves to receive help so long as everyone understands that, given sufficient time, we certainly could have managed on our own. Thus, there is no question of our really needing help due to any sort of personal inability.

The term *interdependence* is used frequently throughout this book. In each case it is at least implied that such a state of mutual love and care between members of Christ's Body is the ideal. Here, again, we must deal with the attitude which holds that any sort of dependency is weakness and that weakness is a bad thing. While it is true that morbid, incapacitating dependency is certainly an indication of an emotional or personality problem, it is equally true that *extreme independence* indicates an equivalent degree of illness. The difference being that one sort of 'illness' is sanctioned, even encouraged, by our culture, and the other is not. In fact, the true state of health for human beings is found in a life-style which involves the individual in interdependent, mutually caring, loving relationships.[3]

What we need to see, at this point, is that many of our ideals, even much of our praying, simply seek the wrong things. We so often seek strength so that we can individually stand and endure, when the Lord would desire to provide a loving, caring brother or sister so that we might stand together. But, before we will be able to accept such a provision from the Lord, we will need to change our ideas and attitudes about dependency itself.

There have been some changes in our cultural attitude to dependency, or 'weakness' as it is often labelled, but these changes fall far short of the values I'm suggesting. For instance, more recently we've come to accept the idea that probably everyone at one time or another needs help; no one can be expected to be absolutely strong at all times. But even such a general acceptance of periodic weakness or need of help has produced a sort of 'double standard' for weakness which says, 'I can still love and respect you if you are weak at times, but I wouldn't be able to love me if I were that weak.' Therefore, the amount of weakness which we can tolerate in others while still respecting them is quite different from the amount of weakness which we can tolerate in ourselves and still have self-respect.

A second idea which results from our more tolerant attitudes about dependency or weakness is that we often class such weakness as an 'illness' which is to be treated like any other illness. That is to say, we can be far more tolerant of weakness, in both ourself and others, if there is evidence that

101

the situation is improving and the person is 'getting well'. By that, we mean that soon the person won't be dependent any more. What we've really come to accept is *temporary* dependency. This attitude can be found in nearly every school of modern therapy or counselling – including Christian counselling. We offer a person help or care until they don't need it any more, because, at the very base of our values, we still believe that the real state of human health is independence! And, because of this basic belief, we continue to develop spiritual or psychological braces and splints in order to enable the individual to stand without support from another human being as our social ideal requires.

Perhaps, at this point, we need to talk about a major fallacy in the very principle of he-man Christianity – in fact, in the whole he-man ideal. Those who would defend he-man Christianity would say that each person needs to be individually strong because that is his *best* defence against any adversity of life or attack on his faith. Furthermore, such individual strength and courage are seen, somehow, to demonstrate a greater self-discipline and, thus, to bring more honour to Christ. And, yet, we have many sayings in our culture which point to a different conclusion: 'divide and conquer'; 'in unity there is strength'; and 'united we stand; divided we fall'. (The scriptural equivalents, to which we've already referred, are: 'it is not good that the man should be alone';' two are better than one'; and 'a threefold cord is not quickly broken', as well as Christ's concern that the Father make us 'one'.) If we simply look at the alternatives, individual strength versus united strength, it's really rather foolish to insist that strong individuals in isolation from one another are really safer from any sort of attack than individuals united in a common strength. And, yet, we have been insistent that the individual Christian is better off when he stands alone in the strength of the Lord.

I think we must be honest enough to admit that we have preferred each individual to stand on his own with Christ because it is ego satisfying not because it offers superior protection! In fact, as a result of our efforts to help each person on his own to realise his 'greatest potential in Christ', individual Christians have been constantly more vulnerable to attack and defeat. How ironic – our 'strength' has become our weakness. The truth which we need to see now is that what we've called 'weakness' in the past is, in fact, our strength. What we need to do is to teach individuals, and the Body of Christ as a whole, how to love and care for one another in mutually caring relationships. Again and again it must be stressed that the ideal state of health for man is in mutually caring, loving relationships which involve *interdependence*, rather than the extremes of either independence or dependence. (We will be talking much more about the health-producing function of loving care within the Body of Christ in chapters nine, ten, and eleven.)

Another attitude which makes receiving difficult comes from the honest belief that only the strong are able to help the weak. Therefore, if we are weak enough to need help from others, we are, obviously, not strong enough to be able to give help to anyone else. Again, the ideal of he-man Christianity is largely responsible for this idea. It is simply inconceivable to most of us that our weaknesses could be of any value to someone in real need of help. This false idea was the very blindness which caused some at the cross to mis-perceive Jesus. They said, 'He saved others; let him save himself' (Luke 23: 35). And, since he did not, they concluded that he had nothing to offer. Notice how forthright Paul is about his own infirmities (2 Cor. 12: 10). But, in accord with our he-man ideal, we reinterpret Paul's statements regarding his infirmities as though they referred to past problems which he had overcome. But a more honest reading of the epistles will reveal certain frailties in Paul which apparently lasted all his life and about which he was most honest and that, when in need, he readily asked for the same sort of loving help and support which he had given to others.

The fact that the Lord could and would use one's weaknesses and problems to help others has been a most difficult lesson for me to learn. From the standpoint of both a clergyman and a psychologist, I'm still amazed every time it happens. About a year after Deb and I came to England, I was, again, one of the speakers at a Post Green Youth Camp. After one of the evening meetings, one of the Bible College students named Andy came and asked if I would take a walk with him so that we could talk. It was a lovely, moonlit summer evening, and we started walking down one of the little Dorset lanes, and Andy began to talk. He said that he was finding it impossible to believe any spiritual issue to be as simple and as uncomplicated as he had at one time. And that meant that he could no longer take most of what he saw and heard at the camp at face value. At some point, he said to me, 'Jim, how do I go back to that simple naïveté of faith that I once had?' What Andy didn't know, at that time, was that I had written a very tear-stained letter to a close friend of mine more than ten years earlier asking him the same question, in almost the same words! That question, coming as it did from Andy in that particular setting, tore open the old scars, and I began to weep. I said to Andy, 'Look, if you want to talk to someone who can give you an answer or who no longer struggles with the same problem, you really need to go to someone else. But, if you want to talk and pray together and let me share the problem with you as one who knows how it feels, I can offer you that.' And so, we walked and talked and prayed together for two or three hours that night, and there was born a love and the beginnings of a relationship between us such that Andy (together with his wife Jill and their babies) is one of the people dearest in my life. We have, since that time, shared life deeply. We've loved and hurt each other, but there is no doubt that God has given us to one another, not because we are each a tower of strength to the other but because love heals and fulfils whether it entails strength or weakness and whether or not it is perfect.

Still another related attitude which makes receiving difficult – which is also related to the idea that the strong give and the weak receive – is the belief that an individual is basically either a 'giver' or a 'receiver'. And, unfortunately, many social roles, as well as many of the ministries in the Church, are seen as requiring givers. Thus, if one wishes to be seen as truly worthy of such distinction, it is important not to be thought of as a receiver. Such an idea is certainly not borne out of the Scriptures. Jesus himself was obviously the giver in many, many situations. Mary, however, anointed his feet and wiped them with her hair, and Jesus took comfort in that love (John 11: 2, see also Luke 7: 37–50). In the garden, it was Jesus who begged Peter, James, and John to stay awake and watch with him. And it was Jesus who sought out Peter to ask him if he still loved him. Paul, too, both gave and received; we've already discussed Paul's need of Timothy and Mark. And, of course, there are his many references to his desire for and need of support and care, especially in prison. He had learnt in all things to be content – as both giver and receiver. What Paul came to know was that he was profitable to his loved ones, and to the Church at large, whether he was giving to them or receiving from them. God help us to accept that truth and to come to believe it in the depths of our hearts so that we can stop playing games with one another and can truly offer ourselves to one another, both to give and to receive.

Earlier in this chapter, while discussing problems associated with giving, we considered the problem of offering only skills or training rather than also giving ourselves. Now, we need to talk about the other side of that problem. It is the expectation on the part of the receiver that one can only receive the help one needs from a 'qualified' giver. This expectation often includes the belief that, when the right helper is found, it will be someone who has 'the answers' to the particular problems involved. While it cannot be denied that there is value in seeking advice now and again, by and large, such ready-made answers are seldom sufficient for most human problems. Real help and real answers to life's problems are most frequently to be found in a developing, sustaining relationship in which we can dare to experience ourselves and in which we can depend on those who love us to care and be both patient and honest with us. However, as long as there are those who insist upon looking for help of a particular sort, the pressure is on those who want to be of help to play out the expected role. The result is that both the giver and the receiver lose out on that which is intended to come to those who love and care for one another in open, honest relationships. Therefore, not only must we learn to give ourselves, rather than only our talents and skills, but we must learn to receive and to appreciate simple love and care and the power which these have to heal and sustain.

The final attitude related to receiving which I would like us to consider is one which follows from the scripturally based teaching which was mentioned briefly in chapter three. Jeremiah 17: 5–8 reads as follows:

Thus says the LORD: 'Cursed is the man who trusts in man and makes flesh his arm, whose heart turns away from the LORD. He is like a shrub in the desert, and shall not see any good come. He shall dwell in the parched places of the wilderness, in an uninhabited salt land. Blessed is the man who trusts in the LORD, whose trust is the LORD. He is like a tree planted by water, that sends out its roots by the stream, and does not fear when heat comes, for its leaves remain green, and is not anxious in the year of drought, for it does not cease to bear fruit.'

This portion of scripture, perhaps more than any other, has been used to suggest that people are not to be trusted and that Jesus himself is the only true friend one can have. The confusion arises when we forget who and what we are. If together we are the Body of Christ and, therefore, members of him and of one another, then, when we open our lives to one another to give and receive love and care and spiritual gifts, it is not the arm of flesh which is being trusted but Jesus Christ himself through his Body. While it is true that we are not to trust man's wisdom, values, or ideas, as these operate independent of God, it does not follow that we are not to love and trust those who are our brothers and sisters with whom we are one in the Body of Christ.

Finally, let us consider two interrelated fears which prevent both giving and receiving within the Church. First, there is the fear of involvement. We've grown so fond of our independence and privacy that anything which might tie us down is considered a threat to our legitimate rights to do and be as we please. I wish here that I could put forward a more popular point of view, but the truth is this: We belong both to Christ and to one another. Christ's last prayer for his disciples and for us was, 'Father ... I do not pray for these only, but also for those who believe in me through their word, that they may all be one; even as thou, Father, art in me, and I in thee, that they also may be in us, so that the world may believe that thou hast sent me' (John 17: 20–1). And the Holy Spirit has been working within the Church to answer that prayer ever since – most especially in this renewal. In any healthy relationship within Christ's Body, each person is both giving and receiving. In such a mutually caring relationship, it is inconceivable that one individual or the other can be available only as and when he pleases. Jesus certainly felt free to insist that Peter, James, and John watch with him and to express disappointment when they did not remain awake with him. The more modern, cultural ideal which holds that true love never asks a person to be or do anything other than he pleases is simply not scripturally sound. True love makes us available to one another, and true love in Christ requires as much involvement with one another as it does with Jesus. (We will talk about the proper balance between freedom and demands in loving relationships in chapter nine.)

The second fear which we must at least mention is the fear of sexual involvement in loving relationships. To the extent that we are talking about loving relationships between adult human beings, the possibility of sexual involvement cannot be ignored. But here, again, we need our attitudes renewed. In our natural families we readily accept deep, loving, non-sexual relationships because our regard for family relationships puts the individuals involved 'out of bounds' where sexual behaviour is concerned. Somehow, a relationship such as brother or sister itself provides an emotional safeguard. Certainly many in the renewed Church are discovering that Christ can give a spiritual brother or sister, or father or mother, with the same sort of emotional safeguard.

We must not be so naïve as to ignore the fact that even the closest family members do sometimes fall into sexual involvement, but such a realisation does not lead us to renounce all family relationships. Rather, the approach in such cases is to deal with the individuals in the particular relationship. Nevertheless, out of the fear of possible sexual misconduct in non-family relationships, we are guilty of fashioning life-styles and structures within the Church which are based on professionalised ministries and casual, 'nodding' acquaintanceships. But the loss in love and health within the Body is incalculable. We simply must believe God for spiritual strength and safeguards *within* loving relationships. Human beings living in self-imposed social isolation is not God's answer to man's sexuality! As a matter of fact, such isolation and loneliness simply produce a more complex pattern of problems. God help us as the Church to become strong enough and honest enough to deal openly with our sexuality without resorting to social isolation and masks of dishonesty.

We have discussed several changes which must come in our shared, cultural attitudes if we as bodies of believers are going to enter fully into the renewal. We have seen that mutually caring, loving, interdependent relationships are vital to both the individual and the message of the Church.

But what are the particular areas in which we are to sustain and to build up one another and what of the hurts which occur in the very process of our imperfect loving? It is to a consideration of these factors that we must now turn our attention.

9. Healing Processes within the Body

Somehow, expressing love causes the love itself to grow and develop; and, in that state of deepening love, we become increasingly vulnerable to hurts from the very one we've come to love more deeply. Furthermore, if a relationship is one to which we have opened ourselves willingly and joyously in the belief that God himself has given it, then disappointment and hurt in that relationship can be both emotionally and spiritually threatening, and the pain can be almost overwhelming. At such a time, any idea that health, wholeness, and true fulfilment of man's very nature is to be found in loving, interdependent relationships seems doubtful, to say the least. In fact, for many of us, the typical reaction to such deep hurt is to retreat, rebuild our defences, determine to never let a thing like that happen again, and attempt to return to a level and style of relating which is something more like the safe, shallow acquaintanceships which are so common to our culture. I am writing these statements out of personal and very painful experience – so painful, in fact, that there were months when I felt I did not dare teach others that they should open themselves to love and to open, honest relationships if it meant that they could be hurt as I had been.

The first lessons in love within the renewal had been fairly simple. I learnt to pray more simply with people, to put my arms around them and really care that they were hurting, and to be generally more open and available. But it's quite a different matter when the Lord begins to bring people into one's life on a more permanent basis. It's one thing to have a more compassionate love for those one meets and ministers to; it's quite another thing to love someone because they've become a part of one's life and family within the Body of Christ. And it is that which began happening to Deb and me when we returned to stay in England and began to share our lives in the community.

As Deb and I opened our lives more fully to loving others, I began to realise more than ever the potential for healing and health that such caring relationships offered, and I travelled throughout Britain (and in California on our return visits there) sharing in the churches the message of loving relationships within the Body of Christ. It was only after I'd seen others, and then Deb and me, get really deeply hurt within the very relationships which the Lord had initially used for so much healing and fulfilment that I found myself questioning the true value and purpose of such ongoing relationships. Our own personal heartache included both deep hurts within the open, loving relationship we had developed with Andy and Jill and a sudden, unexpected redefinition of the structure and terms of commitment within the community which resulted, ultimately, in the scattering of most of those who had become in so many ways family. Those were truly dark days: hurt by those we had loved most deeply, questioning the very basis upon which it had all happened, and unsure that I had anything of real value to teach or share with others in the Church. It had been difficult when, as a young pastor, I'd been disappointed in the Church's approach to human problems. Again, it had been difficult when, after all my work and study, I'd found that psychological approaches to health fell so far short. But this disappointment was the deepest pain I'd ever known. I believed that I had found the answer to life's fundamental hurts, fears, and loneliness in loving relationships within the Body of Christ – with other members of his Body as well as with the Lord himself. But, apparently, even that had been just one more dream.

There were several months during which I only taught on 'safe' subjects in the churches, and I tried, as best I could, to cover up my hurt and disappointment. I simply felt that I could not resume teaching about real love in the Body if there was the possibility that I might encourage others into the same sort of hurt as I had found. The answers to my questions and doubts came rather slowly, but they did come clearly and firmly. The answer to my hurt and disappointment is coming even more slowly; but that, too, is happening – but only as I'm willing to open myself again and to become vulnerable to the possibility of the same sort of hurt all over again.

The answers to my questions and doubts came in two stages. The first was a simple correction that the Holy Spirit had to help me make in my logic. Without ever really putting it into words, I had simply assumed that *true* love itself is a protection from deep or lasting hurt. Therefore, if one does get really deeply hurt, there must have been something wrong with the relationship in the first place; and, probably, one should never have been in the situation or relationship at all. What that implies, of course, is that there was an initial lack of good judgment. If one presses that logic even further, it means: if real hurt has happened and, therefore, one should not have been involved in the first place, doubt is cast on the worth or validity of anything which had seemed of real value in the relationship prior to the hurt. It also suggests that one, obviously, didn't hear the leading of the Lord correctly which, in turn, casts doubt on one's ability to know the leading of the Lord at all! The despair that such thinking produces is almost intolerable. The error in that whole process of thought is in the first basic assumption. The fact is, true love and valid relationships do not prevent deep hurt. The Holy Spirit made that very clear to me as he reminded me of several New Testament relationships in which real hurt had occurred. Certainly Jesus did not wish that he'd never met Peter because Peter denied him, and no one can doubt the pain which that caused both of them. The look on Jesus' face and Peter's tears are testimony to their mutual hurt (Luke 22: 54–62). For that matter, most of the disciples fled the cross, but that fact did not invalidate their calling or Jesus' love for them or, ultimately, their love for him. And, yet, their absence at the cross could scarcely have gone unnoticed by Jesus.

Some of Paul's relationships are equally clear examples of hurt within loving relationships. Paul had been disappointed and hurt by Mark's leaving in the midst of the first missionary journey; and, therefore, he didn't want to take him on the second journey. But Barnabas, who was to have been Paul's companion, wanted to take Mark, and so Paul and Barnabas quarrelled. In the end, Paul took Silas and Barnabas took Mark; and thus ended a beautiful, loving partnership and shared ministry. At that point in time, Paul was estranged from both Mark and Barnabas. Yet, near the end of his life, Paul wrote to Timothy and asked him to bring Mark to him for, says Paul, 'he (Mark) is very useful in serving me' (2 Tim. 4: 11). Certainly the quarrel between Paul and Barnabas does not invalidate their previous ministry or love, and Paul clearly came to think more highly of

111

Mark again. In the same letter to Timothy, Paul speaks of Demas, another of his fellow workers, who left Paul because he was 'in love with this present world' (2 Tim. 4: 10). The hurt which each of these relationships included cannot be denied, but their validity and worth cannot be denied either. Imperfect humans love imperfectly! But that does not mean that we are, therefore, better off without such love. Love need not be perfect to have value or in order to provide the sort of support and care which we are discussing. How thankful we should be for that! Our own love and care could never be of real value to anyone if imperfect love were invalid.

A more shallow teaching on love often suggests that, since human love is imperfect, we should turn away from man as a resource and rely solely on the love of the Lord. The correction needed in that sort of thinking is simply to note that we are never instructed in the Scriptures to turn away from one another in order to trust the Lord; rather, we are to learn to trust the Lord *in* our loving relationships with one another. Furthermore, we must be understanding and forgiving, both of ourselves and others, as we learn our lessons in love. After all, it has been a very long time since the Church walked in these paths. There are few, if any, current models to observe or established patterns to follow in the Church or, for that matter, in the culture at large. We are truly breaking new, or at least renewed, ground. It's not too surprising, then, that we experience some rather hard bumps and bruises as we learn to love one another. One thing we must never forget, however, is that loving relationships, with all their imperfections, are God's gift and provision to us (Eph. 4: 11–16 and Col. 3: 12–17).

The second stage in finding answers to my questions and doubts came more slowly. I could see that even valid and worthwhile relationships did include hurt, but did that mean that one simply took the hurt as an inevitable part of human loving and then waited in each instance for time to heal enough so that one could somehow go on again? That just didn't seem good enough to me! I was still wrestling with these questions when Deb and I needed to visit our family in California. I was still reluctant to share in the churches that which I could not fully endorse, and so I continued to pray that the Lord would help me to understand the full implications of both love and hurt within his Body.

112

As I was praying one day, I said *again* to the Lord, 'I just can't offer people hope for healing and fulfilment in love if I know they're apt to get hurt even more deeply as a result. I simply can't teach people to get hurt.' And immediately the Holy Spirit began to speak to my heart very clearly, and I found myself in very real conversation with the Lord. He said, 'Did you teach your children to walk?', to which I replied, 'Of course I did.' He said, 'Didn't you realise that they would get hurt in the very process of learning to walk?' But before I could answer, the Lord went on to say, 'What have they gained because you risked those hurts and, furthermore, taught them to take such risks themselves?' At that point, my mind went in several directions at once.

I could see just how many risks were involved even in such an apparently simple thing as learning to walk. I realised that all children are bumped and bruised and that some are even maimed for life in their efforts to learn to walk. And yet, it would never have occurred to me to safeguard my children from such dangers by preventing them from walking. Furthermore, I realised that the possibility of injury isn't limited to the learning phase of walking. Even as adults, we may get severely injured because of a mistake in judgment or a collision with some other person or object. And yet, none of these possible dangers, or even past injuries, could persuade any but those suffering from severe emotional disorders to give up walking because of the risks involved. I realised how much of life and the world is available to each of us because we can get ourselves from place to place. And I said to the Lord, 'There's simply too much at stake, a person really can't afford not to walk if it is at all possible.' And he said, 'That's right, and they can't afford not to love either; there's too much at stake.'

Never let it be said that I give up an argument easily, not even when it's with the Lord! And so I said, 'Yes, but the one fact which allowed me to teach my children to walk, even with the certainty of bumped knees and skinned noses, is that I know that bumped knees and skinned noses heal; I know that the human body is designed to heal itself as a natural function.' But, before I could go on, the Lord said, 'Right, and that's how I designed my Body,' to which I replied, 'I don't see much of that healing going on. I'm still as hurt and broken in many ways as I was when the wounds first happened.' And the Lord said, 'If the natural body has

113

a wound that doesn't heal, what does that tell you?' I said, 'That the body itself is not functioning properly to bring about healing.' The Lord continued, 'And what do you do about it?', to which I answered, 'Well, it doesn't do any good to simply treat the injury; you have to deal with the more basic problem. Real healing depends on the proper functions of the body being restored.' Then the Lord said, 'That's right, but what happens if those natural functions of the body are not restored?' I replied, 'Then the range of activity must be restricted so that the risk of wounds is reduced to a minimum.' And the Lord said, 'And that's what has happened to my Body. My people are less and less willing to risk the hurts which can come from deeply loving one another. And their fear, just as yours, is largely because the wounds so often fail to heal.' And then he said, 'Are you prepared to teach about the natural healing functions within my Body in order to help restore them so that my people can love and care for one another without the crippling fear of wounds which do not heal?' At that point, I gave up and said, 'Lord, if you have designed your Body with built-in healing and health producing functions, I simply do not recognise what they are. You'll have to show them to me, if you want me to talk to your Body about them.'

The Lord so often uses such simple ways to confirm his words to us. On the next day after he had spoken to me so clearly, Deb and I received a letter from Paul and Lita, a young couple in England who had also attended Christian Life College. They were now living in Shrewsbury, and their young son, Simeon, was about thirteen months old. Lita's part of the letter began, 'Simeon is black and blue from bumping into things, poor thing, but he can take several steps at a time now.' Somehow, that one sentence seemed to make me more determined then ever to find answers to love and hurt in Christ's Body.

The next several weeks were rather exciting. I decided to read all of the epistles again for any trace of either direct instruction in, or implied reference to, any function within the Body which, if it were available in consistent and dependable ways, would give individual members support and confidence and would be a healing agent. The teaching which follows in this and the next two chapters is the result of that search of the Scriptures, as I asked the Lord to teach me so that I could teach others.

After having talked about love in nearly every chapter of this book, it seems incredible that it should be our starting point again. But love is where we must start the search for healing functions within the Body, not any sort of love or manner of regard but a quality of love which promotes healing of past wounds and provides on-going healing as new wounds occur. How strange that it is love which first opens us to one another, that it is in the process of loving and learning to love more deeply that wounds are incurred, and that it is, then, more love which provides the healing for those very wounds. Such an on-going process is true, however, only when the love involved is of a particular quality.

Before we begin to consider the sort of love which is particularly healing, it may be profitable to review briefly what we have already discussed about love. We began looking at our basic nature created in the image of God and our need to choose love over independence in order to fulfil our nature and to avoid the loneliness and illness which otherwise result. We then discussed the fact that both our culture and the Church have historically adopted a he-man image based upon independence as the proper model of health. We looked next into the cultural revolt and the Church renewal and noted how these two movements are related. We talked about the fact that, in both the culture and the Church, new attitudes regarding love and gentleness are slowly producing a new, more compassionate and honest model of health based upon interdependence. We, then, considered the cost to the individual of such renewal in terms of personal change. Next, we discussed the place of loving relationships within the Body of Christ and how such relationships are a means of healing and fulfilment for the individual. We went on, then, to consider the changes in social attitudes regarding giving and receiving which are necessary before we can sustain on-going, mutually caring relationships. Finally, at the beginning of this chapter, we recognised the problem of deep hurt in close relationships themselves; and, now, we must talk about that sort of love which heals the very wounds of love itself – as well as other truly deep hurts of life.

The significant ingredient which love must have truly to heal and sustain is *affection*. Paul writes, 'Love one another with brotherly affection – as members of one family' (Rom. 12: 10a, The Amplified Bible). It is for this reason that it has been so necessary to insist that we understand that true love includes both *agape* and *phileo*. But the mere *feeling* of affection is not enough either; true affection must be *expressed*. It is for this reason that we needed to talk about our fear of involvement, and especially sexual involvement, because we must come to the place where we can express our love to one another in ways which will provide the necessary affection. Indeed, the New Testament simply assumes that affectionate love will be the norm in the Church.[1]

But even such a description as 'brotherly affection' leaves many of us without any clear understanding of what is being called for, since the expression of real affection is discouraged even between natural brothers as adults throughout most of our culture. We have been taught to fear our emotions so much that we are unable to distinguish between strong healthy emotions and strong unhealthy or destructive ones. This fact means that the Holy Spirit is having to teach many of us who have never before been allowed to be affectionate how to love openly and honestly. It is a lesson which we must not fail to learn because there are times of hurt and pain when there is simply no substitute for a hand to hold: '. . . woe to him who is alone when he falls and has not another to lift him up' (Eccles. 4: 10). Likewise, there are times of gladness when it is just as essential that we have someone with whom to lovingly share and rejoice. It is such a joy to see young people, with fewer 'hang-ups' than our generation, so freely and openly give themselves to Jesus and to one another in this renewal. For instance, it is an incredibly beautiful thing at a youth camp or a retreat to see two young men or two young women strike off across a field with their arms around one another's shoulders, caught up in loving joy. The Church has so much to learn from this new generation!

But such a sight as I've just described should not really surprise us or be unusual in the Church. Our instructions are nearly two thousand years old. Peter writes, 'Now that by obedience to the truth you have purified your souls until you feel sincere affection towards your brother Christians, love one another whole-heartedly with all your strength' (1 Pet. 1: 22, The New English Bible). This scriptural statement includes a third New Testament word for love, *philadelphia*, which means love, fondness, and affection for one's brother. Taken together, the terms for love and the statement itself,

116

the intention is clear: We are to love one another dearly and tenderly with genuine affection as true brothers and sisters. Furthermore, such affectionate love is to be both felt and expressed. The *purpose* or *goal* which Peter cites for having purified our souls is that we may come to feel affection toward one another. I think that very few modern-day Christians would list such a reason if they were asked to say why, that is for what reasons, they became a Christian. Such things as: to find God, to have my sins forgiven, to receive eternal life, or to find real meaning and purpose in life would certainly be named. But how many of us would say that we became Christians so that we could learn to love, and particularly to feel affection, so that we could find brothers and sisters in a new family – the family of God? Since our culture has taught us to be so closed off where affectionate emotions are concerned, it is not too surprising that most of us would not knowingly seek Christ for such a reason. The real tragedy, however, is that few of us, even after we are converted and receive Christ, are ever taught by our churches that this is one of the Lord's prime objectives for us! More often, we are immediately launched in pursuit of individual strength and an individual relationship with the Lord. How desperately we need the Holy Spirit to teach us what a fully balanced life with the Lord and one another is!

Before we leave the more general subject of affection itself to talk more specifically about affection within loving relationships, let's consider the proper *extent* of affection within the Body of Christ. We have already identified at least three fears which are associated with the expression of affection. One is the fear that many people, particularly men in our culture, have regarding the expression of anything which is gentle or tender, because such feelings have been associated with weakness. Another fear has to do with feeling or expressing any strong emotion, since it is feared that such emotions may lead to 'loss of control'. And the third fear is, of course, that of sexual involvement itself. What we must begin to see is that we've denied ourselves a whole range of feelings and experiences in an attempt to guard against excess and extreme. Of course, we do not want, nor does God's Word ever sanction, improper sexual behaviour. But, there is a whole range of loving and caring which must include a hand to hold and an arm which holds and supports and a shoulder to rest or weep on, if ever we are going to be

117

true brothers and sisters and if we are going to love one another as the Scriptures depict true love.

As a matter of fact, Paul goes so far as to instruct, 'Greet one another with a holy kiss' (2 Cor. 13: 12). Paul obviously believed that such a thing was appropriate and that it was possible without leading to misconduct. We, however, have applied our Puritan reasoning to this particular scripture and have concluded that it only applies properly to cultures where such behaviour is already acceptable, as though existing social custom were a better guide to what is good for man than the Scriptures. On the other hand, we do have a reasonable basis for our rejection of such an instruction. We are very aware of something which Paul seems to have overlooked, and that is that some kisses are not holy! How could Paul have been so foolish! Or, is it we who are the foolish ones? Some people overeat – which is the sin of gluttony; do we, then, all stop eating? Some people oversleep; do we all stop sleeping? Individual cases of excess must be dealt with honestly and firmly on scriptural grounds, but to apply blanket prohibitions which deny a quality of life to the whole Body is not protection – it's robbery!

The robbery is even more obvious and painful when we recognise what we're offered in place of true love. Even in churches with the very warmest of atmospheres, the depth of relating is usually rated in terms of 'friendliness' as evidenced by warm handshakes and wholehearted greetings. But all of that, and more, is available at any well-patronised pub. The lost commodity in our culture is not friendliness; it's love – warm, tender, unashamed love. Somehow, the Lord must help us not to be afraid to learn to love with affection and warmth, and he must teach us new boundaries so that we can know and experience the love we need, safe from those things which we know to be sin.

But love and affection which is generally available within the body as a whole is not enough to provide the individual with that love which he needs for personal healing, growth, and fulfilment. While it is lovely to see groups of Christians give one another warm hugs as 'hellos' and 'good-byes', as is true in many fellowships within the renewal, such moments of warmth and affection often only serve to point out to the individual just how devoid of love his day-to-day life really is. Such a stark realisation often causes individuals to become even more guarded, lest they should come to

118

depend upon a certain level of affection and then find themselves in situations where it is not available. Sometimes it seems better to do without a thing altogether than to run such a risk. Therefore, as we consider expressed affection as a means of healing and health within the Body, we must recognise that it is on-going relationships which provide the stable framework for the needed affection. The love and affection which Paul and Timothy had for one another involved far more than warm hellos and good-byes at meetings! They depended upon one another, and they were available to one another. They knew one another well, and it hurt them to be apart. In such a stable relationship, tender affection is as consistently available as human beings are able to be consistent. But, the very idea of consistency and availability brings up yet another problem.

The problem is, of course, our old friend, 'fear of loss of independence'. If we come to need one another's affection, as Paul needed Timothy's, then we'll each need to be there when the other one needs us, or else we'll hurt one another and be disappointed just as Paul was with Demas. Obviously the solution lies in an honest appraisal of our values. And, again, we're right back to choosing love over independence, just as we discussed in chapter two, because that which is gained through love is more valuable than that which is lost in the forfeit of independence! Having said that, however, we must bring a balance by noting that relationships which are truly built on *mutual* care and need provide sufficient room for each person to develop his or her own potentials. Loving, committed relationships are never intended to spend one person for the benefit of the other. And, yet, it cannot be denied that each person must be prepared to lay aside their own self-interests in favour of that which can be discovered and built together. I've often wondered if Timothy ever regretted laying aside whatever it was that he was doing when Paul came through Lystra on his second journey. Apparently Demas had regrets. Surely Demas was the poorer for leaving Paul. Notice that Paul does not say that Demas forsook Christ, only that he had forsaken Paul.

But on-going relationships are not, in and of themselves, all that is needed to provide the individual with dependable love and affection. Human emotions are subject to rather drastic mood shifts; and, thus, a stabilising factor is necessary if love is to be available with any degree of consistency

119

even within the most loving relationship. At this point, we need to remind ourselves that love is a fruit of the Spirit (Gal. 5: 22–3). Therefore, we need not and must not attempt to love one another in our own strength alone. We can expect the Holy Spirit to teach us how to love, to strengthen our ability to love, and to make us consistent in that love. Certainly, it is in this area of our life that the Spirit desires to answer our prayers when we pray to be more like Jesus. I must be frank and say that I have purposely waited until this point in our discussion of love before emphasising that love is a fruit of the Spirit. That is because of the common attitude which holds that the love which is a fruit of the Spirit is a special or 'spiritual' sort of love which does not need to include genuine *feelings* of love. To be sure, love which the Holy Spirit teaches and produces is far more consistent and persistent; but it is warm, tender, affectionate love all the same. Those who are loved by us as we are empowered to love by the Holy Spirit may be aware that our love is particularly dependable, but they will not sense a sort of 'heavenly' love without much 'earthly' substance. We are not robots through whom the Spirit imparts love to the Body and the world. Rather, we are human beings, created in the image of a loving God, whose lives and natures are being conformed to that image by the teaching and the power of the Holy Spirit. It is not that as humans we are unable to love; it is that we love so imperfectly. The Holy Spirit seeks to provide the stability and the guidelines to correct the imperfections in our natural loving by his own strength within us.

Finally, we must discuss one very real hindrance to building loving, affectionate relationships within the Body of Christ. It is a rather informal teaching which is widespread throughout the Church. It holds that each Christian ought to love everyone, and certainly all other Christians, the same. Such an idea automatically reduces all love within the Body to a shallower level, since it is not possible for any one person to build deep, loving relationships with large numbers of people. Furthermore, the whole idea is not scripturally sound. Jesus himself chose twelve who were closer to him than his other followers. Out of the twelve, he very often drew Peter, James, and John closer to him. And finally, there was John who laid his head on Jesus' breast and to whom Jesus gave his mother at the cross. It is true that we must be prepared to love everyone, but we can expect to be drawn into relationships of varying depth with various members of the body. The true measure of our love is that we love everyone, not that we love everyone in the same way or to the same depth.

Deep, loving relationships within the Body do require certain precautions, however. While it is true that we won't love everyone the same, we are to love everyone. Therefore, we must deal openly and honestly with anything which prevents us from loving any particular individual. It is also true that we should not allow our prejudices regarding such things as wealth and status to direct our love toward some and away from others (Jas. 2: 1–7). We must also be careful that individuals are not left out and made to feel excluded, as closer relationships form within the Body. But, again, the solution is not to be found in penalising the whole for the sake of those who find entering into relationships difficult. In our effort to equalise and bring uniformity, we have once again distorted Christianity until it is barely recognisable in its present form. Can you imagine anyone correcting Jesus and John because Thomas or Nathaniel might have felt left out, or Paul and Timothy or Paul and Luke because others might have felt excluded? The solution is not to deny close, caring, affectionate relationships in order to prevent hurt or exclusion; rather, we need to be taught how to have *open* relationships. Loving relationships within the Body need to be open and available to others, not exclusive – *all* relationships, including marriage. Furthermore, true love must be talked about and taught about such that loving relationships will once again become available to each member of the body. First-century Christians were terribly clannish and very prone to give themselves to loving, committed relationships; and the world marvelled and said, 'See how these Christians love one another.' God help us to cause them to say that again!

So far, in our discussion of healing and health within the Body, we've talked only about love, and particularly affection. It is right to give affectionate love itself such a prominent place in our discussion (Col. 3: 12–17), but there are many other related functions of the Body which we must also consider, and it is these which we will discuss in the next two chapters.

10. More about Healing Processes within the Body

In our discussion of affectionate love as the most basic healing function within the Body, we noted a distinction between the general presence of love within the Body as a whole and that love which is directly available to the individual through specific, on-going relationships which are both stable and dependable. We must continue to bear in mind that same distinction throughout all of our discussion of the various healing functions within the Body. That is to say, it is not enough for individuals to relate on a general level to a somewhat nebulous body of believers. For true healing and health, we must care for, and be cared for by, those with whom we have mutual, interdependent relationships. Such relationships are to be marked by a depth of affection and openness and are the chief vehicle through which the world sees Christians loving one another.

Let us turn now to a further consideration of truth and truthfulness. In discussing the cultural revolution and Church renewal, we noted that there is a growing tendency to want to discard the socially approved masks which we typically wear. It is important, at this point, to discuss how discarding social masks is related to healing and good health. It would seem that within the human heart there is a basic need to be known for just what we are and not what we appear to be. Basil Dowling expresses that longing in these words:

> With 'No Admittance' printed on my heart,
> I go abroad, and play my public part;
> And win applause – I have no cause to be
> Ashamed of that strange self that others see.
>
> But how can I reveal to you, and you,
> My real self's hidden and unlovely hue?
> How can I undeceive, how end despair
> Of this intolerable make-believe?

You must see with God's eyes, or I must wear
My furtive failures stark upon my sleeve.[1]

The scriptural position on the issue of self-disclosure versus deceit is clear: We *must* wear our furtive failures stark upon our sleeves! Paul writes: 'Do not lie to one another, seeing that you have put off the old nature with its practices' (Col. 3: 9) and 'Therefore, putting away falsehood, let every one speak the truth with his neighbour, for we are members one of another' (Eph. 4: 25).

The task of learning to be honest with one another is not a simple one. Our culture has sanctioned so much deceit in the name of 'good manners' or 'good breeding'. When we say, 'Good morning, how are you?', we don't really expect the other person to tell us. We are simply exchanging a greeting to which they are to reply, 'Just fine, thank you.' Even amongst those who have truly sought to be more open and honest, there is a tendency for such openness to be somewhat selective. I recall a time in our life together in the community when smaller groups of us regularly shared many of our belongings and, also, much of our inner-selves – our hopes and dreams as well as past hurts and disappointments. And, still, we found it incredibly difficult to tell one another truthfully if we did not have enough money to pay our electricity bill! Somehow, that sort of honesty was 'out of bounds'.

It is impossible to overstress the need for honesty if we are going to be fully whole people. Paul Tournier says, 'No one can develop freely in this world and find a full life without feeling understood by at least one person ...' I suppose that psychology and psychiatry, as professions, are particularly aware of the problem of people locked up inside themselves with no one who really knows them, much less loves them, for just what they are. The heart cry comes through rather 'loud and clear' when one deals with people who come for counsel or help. I am both saddened and embarrassed by the fact that the Church has done so little to release people from the fears which hold them behind bars of deceit especially in light of the prophetic commission of Christ and his Church:

The Spirit of the Lord GOD is upon me, because the LORD has anointed me to bring good tidings to the afflicted; he has sent me to bind up the brokenhearted, to proclaim liberty to the captives, and the opening of the prison to those who are bound . . . to comfort all who mourn . . . to give them a garland instead of ashes, the oil of gladness instead of mourning (Isa. 61: 1–3).

Relatively few 'prison doors' in this world are made of iron, and we who have been sent forth to set at liberty the captive have, in fact, actually helped to fashion many of the doors.

How desperately the Church needs this current renewal! Openness and honesty provide the only real solution to the very difficult problem of people locked away within themselves. And we have both the instruction and the privilege to live open, honest lives with one another on an on-going basis. Again, it must be pointed out that it is within the framework of a loving relationship that such openness and honesty are most successfully accomplished. One of the fears which prevents so many of us from being more honest about ourselves is the fear that, when others know the truth, they'll leave. Loving, committed relationships in which trust has been built-up serve to counteract that fear. I am more grateful than I have words to express for those who know me and love me for just what I am, without demanding pretence on my part. They are the richest treasure I have on earth! And, because we are members together of Christ's Body, our love for one another extends beyond the limits of this present life on earth into the eternal.

But there is another important factor about honesty with one another which must be discussed. It is the fact that we cannot truly know ourselves until someone else is willing to know us as we are. Paul Tournier writes, 'He who would see himself clearly must open up to a confidant freely chosen and worthy of such trust.' We have such misconceptions about ourselves until we see ourselves reflected in the responses of others. But, we can't take a chance on the nature of their responses, unless we know and trust their love. And yet, we can't know and trust their love if we haven't ventured out, at least a little. It is this rather difficult bind which gives rise to the sort of 'start – stop' procedure which most enduring relationships go through in the early stages of development. In psychology, it is referred to as 'building bridges of trust'. It means simply that we venture a little and then pull back just slightly and wait for a favourable response before we venture further.

The process of building bridges of trust, or establishing ties, is rather frightening to most of us. Hurts come so quickly and easily when we offer ourselves to one another. There is a touching scene in *The Little Prince* by Antoine de Saint-Exupéry which depicts the rather fearful way we approach each other. In this scene, the Little Prince has just met the fox who explains that he cannot play with the Little Prince because he is not tamed:

LITTLE PRINCE: What does that mean – 'tame'?

FOX: It is an act too often neglected. It means to establish ties . . . Please – tame me!

LITTLE PRINCE: I want to, very much. But I have not much time. I have friends to discover, and a great many things to understand.

FOX: One only understands the things that one tames. Men have no more time to understand anything. They buy things all made at the shops. But there is no shop anywhere where one can buy friendship, and so men have no friends any more. If you want a friend, tame me . . .

LITTLE PRINCE: What must I do, to tame you?

FOX: You must be very patient. First you will sit down at a distance from me – like that – in the grass. I shall look at you out of the corner of my eye, and you will say nothing. Words are the source of misunderstandings. But you will sit a little closer to me, every day . . .[2]

I suppose that past hurt and rejection won't let us build relationships without such a testing of one another, but we do need the Lord to help us get on with the process so that we can come quickly to know one another and ourselves and to move on into healing and a more fulfilling life together.

The final factor we must talk about in relation to truth and honesty within Christ's Body is the required relationship between truth and love. Paul writes, '. . . speaking the truth in love, we are to grow up in every way into him who is the head, into Christ, from whom the whole body, joined and knit together by every joint with which it is supplied, when each part is working properly, makes bodily growth and upbuilds itself in love' (Eph. 4: 15–16). These two dynamics modify each other: Love without truth is dangerous, and truth without love is deadly. As we love one another, we must keep before us that which we know to be true of one another so that each may carefully protect the other – often from himself. We must keep in mind the truth of God's Word so that our love remains honourable and healing. Likewise, we must temper such truth with love. We have a saying in our culture: 'The truth never hurt anyone.' That saying is a lie! The truth, ruthlessly used, has killed some people. The truth *in love* is a healing scalpel in a surgeon's hand. The truth *without love* is a weapon of destruction. It is, after all, only love which gives us the scriptural right to speak the truth to one another. Without love, we are to keep silent since it is love which determines whether truth and honesty heal or destroy. Another of Graham Kendrick's songs sums up this scriptural principle in these words:

> You say you speak the truth and so you do
>   Your finger points and spares no pain
> But where were the love and tears that earned the right to wound
>   Learn to love, then speak the truth and gain a friend.
>
> You've been taking without giving
>   Giving without loving
> Hurting without healing up the wounds
>   Forgiven yet not forgiving.[3]

The next function of the Body which heals and provides stability for the individual is the actual support we are to be to one another. What a strange twist of doctrine it is which regularly reminds believers that they are to 'bear one another's burdens', while just as regularly instructing them not to rely on help from any man and to take their burdens only to the Lord. If that rather 'schitzy' teaching were to be followed to the letter, it would mean, of course, that everyone would be offering loving care and help to others; but no one would be taking it! What actually does happen very often is that those who are strong in a particular situation help the weaker ones with that strange mixture of humility and virtue which comes from doing those things for others which others 'really ought to be doing for themselves', while those who receive the help are plagued by a sense of personal unworthiness and of having failed in faith. Let us look to see just what the Scriptures do say.

Paul writes: '. . . through love be servants of one another . . . Bear one another's burdens, and so fulfil the law of Christ' (Gal. 5: 13 and 6: 2). Note that it has been necessary to talk about honesty before we could talk about bearing one another's burdens. The Scriptures simply assume that we will know what one another's burdens are. Note, also, that our need of one another is taken for granted. What a source of comfort and reassurance it is when we know that there are those who love us and will help to shoulder our load when we grow weary – for whatever reason. The principle of healing in these instructions is clear. The offer is for rest and relief from the strain of the burden. How well we understand this need in the physical realm. The recommended treatment for even a minor illness is proper food, proper sleep, and *above all* rest. It is simply understood that the physical body needs time away from exertion in order to rebuild itself. I do wish that we were more ready to relieve one another of the strain of the full weight of our burdens and labours in other spheres of life so that we could be built-up in the faith and rested in our souls. Many Christians break under the unnecessary attempt to cope with all of life on their own because they think that a 'good Christian' ought to be able to do so. In every area of our life together, we need to be sensitive to respond when any one of us needs relief from accumulated pressures. As members of the Body of Christ and of one another, we are not interchangeable units to be used up, disposed of, and replaced. God forgive us for our abuse of ourselves and of one another in the name of dedication.

There is, however, a limit to the extent of the 'help' we are to be to one another. Paul declares, 'But let each one test his own work, and then his reason to boast will be in himself alone and not in his neighbour. For each man will have to bear his own load' (Gal. 6: 4–5). It seems almost contradictory that these words of Paul should follow almost immediately after his instruction to bear one another's burdens. The balance, however, which these complementary instructions offer is vitally important. While we must always help one another as we each cope with our own responsibilities and calling, we must never attempt to relieve

127

any individual of his God-given right to be responsible in the kingdom of God. One person must never attempt to take over the responsibility for any decision, duty, or calling from another member of the Body. We are to *share* in the bearing of each other's burdens. Such sharing never displaces any individual but rather makes available to all the resources of their combined gifts. Thus, when we help bear each other's load, we truly serve – and are God's gift to – one another. If any individual, or group of individuals, moves into another person's place, no matter how noble the motive, they are not helping that person; they are robbing him. Such 'help' produces protégés of men rather than disciples of Jesus. Furthermore, each individual will, finally, have to stand before the Lord to give an account of his own life and calling. No one in that day will be able to stand to defend another for having lived his life under their directives. I do wish that those who are teaching such strong positions on 'authority and submission' and 'discipling' would see a balance between that which we *must do* for one another in order to fulfil the law of Christ and that which we *must not do* to any child of God, before more damage is done in the name of commitment and renewal.

There is another direct instruction that we are to bear one another's burdens: 'Those of us who have a robust conscience must accept as our own burden the tender scruples of weaker men, and not consider ourselves. Each of us must consider his neighbour and think what is for his good and will build up the common life. For Christ too did not consider himself . . .' (Rom. 15: 1–3, NEB). This instruction is in direct reference to those who are 'weak in the faith', and it lays a particular burden on those more mature Christians whose conscience is not troubled on various matters. Again, there is a need for balance. Such balancing instructions are found in the fourth chapter of Ephesians which says that, ultimately, we are all to grow up! The dilemma of that which is right for those who are strong or more mature and that which is right for those who are weak or young is a problem faced by every parent as they raise their family. It is the problem of how to enjoy the rights and privileges of an adult without doing injustice to children who lack experience and have less mature understanding. In practical terms, it means being careful for the growing child's welfare and, little by little, introducing him into situations requiring more mature judgment and understanding. The dual duties are clear: The weaker have the right to expect the strong to be patient, loving, and unselfish; and the strong have the right to expect the weaker to be growing up! When one reads through Paul's writings on various subjects such as meat offered to idols and circumcision, one finds the balance between these two expectations interwoven throughout his instructions. In terms of health producing functions within the Body, the particular contribution that this caring of the stronger for the weaker promotes is clear. It is the security which comes to the less mature, developing Christian because he can expect his more mature brothers and sisters to be aware of his well-being and to be prepared to put his welfare before their own liberty.

There is one other issue concerning appropriate standards for weaker Christians which must be considered before we move on. 'Pharisaism' is not dead; it is alive and well in the Church of the Lord Jesus Christ! According to the modern version, any restriction or deprivation is bound to result in a more dedicated, disciplined Christian, as though there were some virtue in sheer discipline for discipline's sake. God has never set standards just to see how much obedience he could get out of man. The doing or the not doing of a particular thing has value only in so far as the thing itself is relevant to man's spiritual well-being. When the principle that discipline in any form is a good thing is used to determine both how we ought to live and how we ought to relate to the weaker members of the Body, it comes out something like this: It is good and right that all Christians should live according to the rules and standards appropriate for the weakest members since such restrictions are, obviously, a measure of the purest life possible. Certainly, Paul never intended his instructions that the stronger should bear the burdens of the weaker to indicate that the rules and standards designed to support the weaker, less mature believers were the best model for godliness. 'If with Christ you died to the elemental spirits of the universe, why do you live as if you still belonged to the world? Why do you submit to regulations, "Do not handle, Do not taste, Do not touch" (referring to things which all perish as they are used), according to human precepts and doctrines? These have indeed an appearance of wisdom in promoting rigour of devotion and self-abasement and severity to the body, but they are of no value, serving only to indulge the flesh' (Col. 2: 20–3). *The Living Bible* translates that last phrase: 'They only make him proud.' It is true that we will be more loving, and certainly more obedient in our care for the weaker ones, if we are careful not to make them stumble; but we will not be more spiritual as a result of those *things* which we do or do not do on their behalf.

Let us now turn to some very practical matters. At some point, if we truly love and care for one another, our provision for each other will become very tangible. What are the scriptural guidelines for the distribution of goods and finance within the Body of Christ and how do these relate to healing and health? We must start by considering the instructions concerning work. 'Let the thief no longer steal, but rather let him labour, doing honest work with his hands, so that he may be able to give to those in need' (Eph. 4: 28). (Note that it is assumed that there will be those in need.) Carrying that instruction further, Paul writes: '. . . when we were with you, we gave you this command: If any one will not work, let him not eat. For we hear that some of you are living in idleness, mere busybodies, not doing any work. Now such persons we command and exhort in the Lord Jesus Christ to do their work in quietness and to earn their own living' (2 Thess. 3: 10–12). The basic principle, then, is that each man is to work if he is able; otherwise, he is not to eat.

Even in ideal situations where all able members are working, we are faced with the problem of the inequalities in human society and the labour market. The instruction as to what to do about such inequalities is found in Paul's second letter to the Corinthians (2 Cor. 8: 8–15). He begins by saying that his instructions are not given as a command but rather as a measure by which to prove genuine love. Paul then presents what he calls 'a matter of equality'. In principle, it says that the abundance of one should supply the want of another in order that there might be equality amongst the members of the body. He gives an example from Exodus regarding the gathering of manna: 'He that gathered much had nothing over, and he that gathered little had no lack' (Exod. 16: 18). To summarise, Paul is saying that all should work and that all should have enough and that none should have a surplus while others who work have less or are in need. It must be pointed out, again, that this is not a command from Paul. It is a plan for the outworking of love. If one tries to organise such a principle into law, the result is some sort of imposed communism. God forbid! But, when this principle serves as a guideline for the outworking of love, such things as money, belongings, goods and even property change hands as needed in the most tender and reassuring ways.[4]

But what does such a principle of practical sharing have to do with healing and health? It is a well-known fact that insecurity is one of the major factors behind many neurotic behaviour patterns. Many of the more common defence mechanisms which modern psychology has identified serve as a means by which the individual attempts to deal with his fears of the unknown and the untried. Life itself can often be perceived as threatening, and the world can seem a very hostile place, especially for those who feel that they have not yet 'established' themselves. The rising popularity of insurance and retirement schemes is an indication of how threatening tomorrow's unknown possibilities can seem. Within the Church, one often hears criticism of those who seem to be too 'security minded', especially if such an attitude interferes with an individual's pursuit of a ministry or of other acts of faith. But the Church is in no position to criticise those who seem to be security minded, if the Church is not prepared to be mindful of their security! Paul could write to the Corinthians and put them in mind of their promises and intentions on his behalf in the confidence that that which they had in abundance should lovingly be shared with him in his time of need. The health value of such a sense of security within a loving family would not be underestimated by any leading school of psychology or psychiatry today!

At this point, we must discuss a related attitude which will need to be corrected if we are ever to be very consistent in sharing material things with one another. John Calvin and the Puritans must both be credited with helping to create an attitude of disdain for the poor. Somehow, prosperity and 'election' or prosperity in material things and the prosperity of the soul became theologically linked. The poor, therefore, were poor either through their own laziness or because God had in some way abandoned them to the consequences of their own folly. But this thinking in no way reflects the scriptural attitude toward the poor. God seems compassionately aware that human systems of labour and reward are imperfect at best and are very often cruel and indiscriminate. It is, therefore, the poor to whom Jesus has promised the kingdom of God (Luke 6: 20) and to whom he preached his Gospel (Luke 4: 18). Further, it is interesting to note that, when Paul and Barnabas went to Jerusalem and were commissioned to preach to the Gentiles the single admonition from James and John was that they, Paul and Barnabas, were to remember the poor. This single instruction regarding the poor becomes even more significant if we recall the number of issues over which the 'Jewish' Christians and the 'Gentile' Christians differed. There are so many other things which Paul and Barnabas might have been encouraged to include in their presentation of the Gospel, that there is little room to doubt the importance placed upon the care of the poor within the early Church (Gal. 2: 9–10). Finally, note again how James shames those in the early Church who did discriminate on the basis of wealth and status (Jas. 2: 1–9). It is no shame for an honest worker to be in want or to be poor, but shame on those believers who are indifferent to want and need within the body, the very Body of Christ. What a tragic loss both to those who might give and to those who might receive, and what a tragic loss to the world who might see Christians truly loving one another.

Another matter which is closely related to the sharing of our goods and belongings is that of hospitality. Again, the Scriptures are clear in their intentions: 'Practise hospitality ungrudgingly to one another' (1 Pet. 4: 9) and 'Contribute to the needs of the saints, practise hospitality ... Welcome one another, therefore, as Christ has welcomed you ...' (Rom. 12: 13 and 15: 7). Notice first that we are to welcome as we've been welcomed. The songs and poems which have been written about heaven being our home would fill volumes. And yet, heaven is actually the abiding place of God himself. We call it our home only because he has opened his home to us and made us welcome there: 'In my Father's house are many rooms; if it were not so, would I have told you that I go to prepare a place for you?' (John 14: 2). How can we, then, close our homes to one another?

Notice further that our giving to one another is intended to be within the bounds of our homes. We are so prone to do whatever we do for one another in ways which are church-building centred. It is for this reason that much of our sharing is so shallow. Modern church buildings are designed to house certain religious functions most of which have little or nothing to do with the family of the Lord getting together and coming to know and love each other. Someone has said, 'A meeting is where no one meets.' How sad that so much of modern Christianity is centred in 'meetings'.

Life in the early Church often centred around the homes of the believers (Acts 2: 46, Rom. 16: 5, Col. 4: 15, and Philem. 2). As a matter of fact, hospitality is rated so highly in the Scriptures that individuals were not considered eligible for leadership within a church body who were not given to hospitality (1 Tim. 3: 20 and Titus 1: 8). I wonder how many local church offices would be filled today if that requirement were enforced? The real loss is, of course, in the quality of our life together. There is a particular quality of warmth which a home setting adds to sharing, conversation, and even to prayer which is lost in other settings. It was a real revelation to me that so many people found it far easier to open themselves up to me with a teatowel in their hands drying the dishes I was washing, than they found it in a proper counselling session with the desk and side lamp neatly in place.

But the Lord really did have to teach Deb and me how to open our home, as well as our hearts, to people. We had had a lovely, large home in California. I, particularly, am very fond of antiques; and so our home had been the setting for as many lovely old things as we could afford – china, art glass, crystal, and furniture. In our 'living room' we had had chairs which had been restored on which *no one* sat! Then, we sold our home and moved to England as the Lord directed us. When we arrived, we were given the use of a small cottage on the Post Green estate. It had not been lived in for a few years and needed a great many repairs, as well as complete redecoration. The Lord began immediately to provide the furnishings we needed to keep house, and many of them were lovely, older pieces. But there was one major difference between these old things and those which we'd had in California – everything here was 'pre-distressed'. We didn't have to worry about getting the first water ring on the table or the first scratch on the tea trolly; they were already there! Furthermore, a series of minor mishaps and misjudgments meant that the new carpet was slightly damaged and the pattern in the new curtains was slightly askew, not to mention that the new floor in the bathroom had to be completely laid twice! These mishaps were all the more ironic since we were accustomed to doing up furnishings and to decorating and had never had anything really spoiled before.

Finally, I said to Deb, 'Do you suppose the Lord is trying to tell us something?' The answer to that question became increasingly clear over the next few months. The Lord began to furnish our home with people and little by little taught us how to relax and enjoy both the things he'd given us and the people. I suppose I'd thought that he'd given us a lovely Wilton carpet because it felt so good to wiggle our toes in; I found out that it was because such things as coffee and orange squash washed out so easily! I don't suppose any of us consciously choose things over people, but our typical life-style makes that choice a fact just the same.

The actual contribution which hospitality makes to healing and health is in the area of 'belonging'. To the extent that our homes are open to one another, every member of the family has available to him a warm welcome and comfort regardless of the individual's particular situation at that moment. The Son of Man may not have had 'a place to lay his head' in terms of a deed of ownership; but, when he was in Bethany, he was at home with Mary, Martha, and Lazarus. Please note that we're not discussing here good deeds done as a ministry to the needy of this world. We're talking about the family lovingly sharing amongst themselves all of the blessings which the Lord has provided jointly for them. The charge that we are to be good neighbours to the poor and broken-hearted of this world – in the fashion of the Good Samaritan – is an equally valid, but different, instruction to the Body of Christ.

To this point, we have considered the rather more serious facets of shared life in the Body of Christ having to do with bearing one another's burdens and concerns and the means by which true love and care heal and sustain the individual. We need now to consider a different facet of our shared life, and that is our shared joy and the way in which shared joy strengthens the individual. 'If one member suffers, all suffer together; if one member is honoured, all rejoice together' (1 Cor. 12: 26). The idea of shared joy is, of course, part of the even larger subject of gladness and light-heartedness, or even such a simple idea as people having a good time together. Somehow, our rather stern image of God has made it nearly impossible for us, as Christians, to feel free to be too happy. Along with our tendency to emphasise the strong, independent side of man's nature, we have also tended to emphasise God's wrath and judgment. That emphasis has been so strong that many Christians find it almost impossible to relate to God as a tender, loving father. What a strange theology such an attitude suggests: If God is only stern and solemn and serious, and we are made in his image, then it must follow that everything about man which enjoys fun and laughter and is light-hearted and tender is the result of sin and the fall – such foolishness!

The Scriptures are clear as to the rightful place of joy and gladness, and even merriment, in human nature and life: 'All the days of the afflicted are evil, but a cheerful heart has a continual feast' (Prov. 15: 15) and 'A cheerful heart is a good medicine, but a downcast spirit dries up the bones' (Prov. 17: 22). Since it's medicine which we are looking for in terms of healing and health, we dare not overlook this commodity. It means that we'll have to develop whole new attitudes and ideas about what is appropriate for Christians to do, particularly when they come together. We are often prone to judge the merit of time spent together in terms of its productivity, and we are very conscious of 'wasted time'. That we ever came to believe that the time spent with the people we love is wasted time, unless some measurable product results, is a sad case of misguided zeal. Actually, there is an even more subtle side to the problem. Because we haven't learnt to play and relax together, we often find that we have to escape from one another in order to be able to really let our hair down and be ourselves. How will we ever share our joys and laughter with each other if we're embarrassed and ashamed to admit to one another that we, too, enjoy a good giggle now and then?

Not only is a cheerful heart a good medicine, but 'the joy of the LORD is your strength' (Neh. 8: 10). How sad that we've robbed ourselves of a major resource of spiritual strength in the name of piety; and for that cause many are weak and sick amongst us. A downcast spirit indeed dries up the bones!

Our carefulness not to be frivolous and waste time is undoubtedly responsible, in part, for our failure to build strong, loving relationships with one another. We accept, almost without question, the idea that two people who love

135

one another in the traditional sense will enjoy being together and that they will significantly increase each other's joy by virtue of simply being with one another. And yet, by and large, we have failed to apply that idea to relationships within the Body of Christ. Somehow, we demand more 'spiritual' reasons for the time and energy we spend together and can actually feel guilty if we enjoy one another's company too much. One of the main reasons that the world sees such shallow love amongst believers is that we have grown accustomed to such shallow relationships and find it almost impossible to justify the time it takes to build relationships of a deeper quality. If we are to love one another fully, the Holy Spirit is going to have to help us develop a whole new set of values, one which places love for one another above other, more 'acceptable' pursuits.

Another factor which interferes with our rejoicing together is, of course, jealousy. It's often camouflaged as self-incrimination. When we first hear of some wonderful thing which has happened to another member of the body, we often respond with real rejoicing, which can be followed very quickly, however, by the question: 'What's wrong with me?' It isn't that we want the honour or the blessing instead of the other person; we just want a share for ourselves as well. This 'me-too-Lord' attitude includes callings and ministries within the Church as well as more tangible provisions. I must confess that, when I hear of great crowds gathering to hear another minister or of miraculous healings, I can very quickly begin to ask, 'What's wrong with me, Lord?'

This particular form of jealousy requires a real change of attitude. We must begin to see the Body of Christ as God sees it, as a real body with mutually interdependent members. Therefore, '. . . if one member is honoured, all rejoice together.' God takes for granted that my joy is fulfilled when he honours any one member of the Body. The real problem is that we cut ourselves off from a major source of joy when we can't rejoice in one another's honours and blessings; and, when that happens, our strength is accordingly reduced. Again, we find a parallel situation in Christ's relationships with his disciples. How do you suppose the other nine felt when Peter, James, and John were so often invited by Jesus to go with him just a bit further? How deeply and fully we will need to love one another if we are ever to be able to accept another's honour as our own, but how strong in our soul we will be as the result!

Throughout this chapter, we have discussed various functions of the Body by which the individual member is both healed and sustained in health. In the following chapter, let us turn our attention to the whole area of the believer's struggle with sin. Often it is the individual's inner conflicts themselves which bring him so much anxiety and fear. Some of our most serious wounds are, after all, self-inflicted. What healing is provided for these?

11. The Sin Problem and the Healing Processes

'As Christians, we're all a bit "schitzy".' I don't know how many times I've said that to my classes at Bible College as we've wrestled with the whole issue of regeneration. That we who have accepted Christ as our Saviour and Lord are new creations being conformed to the image of Christ is a clear teaching of the Scriptures (2 Cor. 5: 17 and Eph. 4: 13). That we, as sons of God, possess eternal life and are even now seated together with Christ in heavenly places is equally well documented (John 17: 3, Eph. 2: 4–7, and 1 John 3:2). However, that we possess these treasures in an 'earthen vessel' which is currently in a corruptible state is equally true (1 Cor. 15: 51–7 and 2 Cor. 4: 7). And it is also true that we war against the law of sin in our natural bodies and long, while the whole of creation longs with us, for the final work of adoption, the redemption of our bodies (Rom. 7: 21–5 and Rom. 8: 19–25). As long as we are in our bodies of flesh, each of us will wage a running battle with natural inclinations which are not Christ-like or godly. Such inclinations run the full course from our human way of looking at things or our attitudes which are simply too restricted to do justice to the things of God on the one hand to the vilest of sins on the other. In our rather simple way of understanding, we often feel that we are, somehow, more spiritual when the more obvious sins are eliminated from our habit patterns. The thing we must see, however, is that it is really a matter of degree. No sooner do we get one bit of behaviour, or an attitude, under control than we become aware of other factors in us which also require attention and even drastic change if we are to continue to develop spiritually. And so shall it ever be until this corruptible has put on incorruption.

The shame is not that we each struggle with a carnal nature; it is that we've made it a secret battle. Stiff-upper-lip Christianity has required that we maintain a mask of respectability, calm, and control regardless of the state of our inward struggle. In order to keep up the façade, we are constantly improving our 'public mask' or 'testimony' and, thereby, heaping guilt on one another because the masks have become so believable. Furthermore, since most people's public masks stay so firmly in place and are, therefore, so often accepted as the truth, we can very easily feel that we must be the only one who faces certain problems and desires and that our mask is the only 'face' which is false.

There are at least three major consequences of this 'cover-up' approach to dealing with our carnal nature. The most obvious, of course, is that the problems remain hidden and are never really dealt with fully. Another is that we deny ourselves the mutual benefits of bearing one another's burdens; in our attempt to manage on our own, we defraud one another of our rightful functions within the body. And finally, the world is denied an honest picture of the Christian experience; and, far from being helped by our carefully controlled testimony, they're sickened by the phony games that we think we're getting by with. The alternative, on the other hand, means that we must be prepared to be honest with one another in areas which have in the past remained safely hidden. To do so will require that somehow we are assured, in advance, of one another's continued love and respect, even after we know the truth about each other. Such assurance will require that we love one another with an 'unconditional' love, the sort of love Jesus has for us.

In 1 John 1: 5–2: 12, we find a very straightforward description of the current state of the believer. John first tells us that God is light and that, if we walk in the light as he is in the light, we have fellowship with one another, and the blood of Jesus cleanses us from all sin. The reason why John says that we have fellowship with one another if we walk in the light is made perfectly clear if we consider John's definition of 'walking in the light'. 'He who says he is in the light and hates his brother is in darkness still. He who loves his brother abides in the light, and in it there is no cause for stumbling' (1 John 2: 9–10). After John's description of the believer's walk in the light – cleansed from sin and in fellowship with Christ and one another – he says, 'If we say we have no sin, we deceive ourselves, and the truth is not in us' (1 John 1: 8). Notice that 'walking in the light' is related to our love for one another and not to a state of sinless obedience or even discipline. John then sums up by saying that his purpose for writing these things is so that we may not sin. But, if we do sin, we are to confess that sin to our advocate, Jesus Christ the righteous; and he will forgive us our sins and cleanse us from all unrighteousness.

We need to talk, at this point, about the whole principle of confession.[1] Since private confession of sins to a human intermediary has played such a dominant role in doctrinal controversy throughout Church history, the term itself has become rather controversial. But the act of confession need not be a formal one or, in fact, a 'religious duty' at all. James tells us to confess, or admit, our sins to *one another* and to pray for *one another* so that we may be healed (Jas. 5: 16). The principle is really rather simple. As we noted first in chapter two, the intended state for man is to have a right and loving relationship with God and right and loving relationships with man. Right and loving relationships are honest and open and free from deceit. Any psychiatrist or psychologist will confirm the health producing effects of such openness and honesty. Therefore, the 'confession' we're looking for within the body is found in on-going, honest sharing within the stable framework of loving relationships – with Christ *and* with one another. Our confession to Christ provides forgiveness of sin as well as maintaining a healthy relationship with him. Our mutual confession to one another, and the involvement in each other's life which that entails, is intended to provide each member with consistent love and care. It must be stressed that it is a loving relationship which provides the basis for such mutual confessions and that neither church hierarchy nor ministries and callings, in and of themselves, determine the appropriate combinations for such confessions. It must also be stressed that confession is always intended to produce restoration, not punishment or rejection. Restoration is the goal even in the most extreme cases of misconduct. 'My brethren, if any one among you wanders from the truth and some one brings him back, let him know that whoever brings back a sinner from the error of his way will save his soul from death and will cover a multitude of sins' (Jas. 5: 19–20). This work of restoration is the carrying out of the work of the Good Shepherd amongst us.

Mutual confession, at its most basic level, is simply the application of the principle of openness and honesty to the sin problem. While openness and honesty are obviously

140

necessary if we are to confess our sins to one another, the full work of restoration requires that the *response* to any confession includes at least two additional factors: (1) scriptural correction and (2) a particular set of attitudes. Scriptural correction means that we lovingly and faithfully remind one another of the scriptural truths which apply in any particular case. 'Rather, speaking the truth in love, we are to grow up in every way into him who is the head, into Christ, from whom the whole body, joined and knit together by every joint with which it is supplied, when each part is working properly, makes bodily growth and upbuilds itself in love' (Eph. 4: 15–16). It must be emphasised that *truth* is not measured by cultural ideals or even our own best intentions but by the Word of God. 'All scripture is inspired by God and profitable for teaching, for reproof, for correction, and for training in righteousness, that the man of God may be complete, equipped for every good work' (2 Tim. 3: 16–17). Remember, however, that even scriptural truth must be spoken in love. The intent is healing not punishment or destruction. Notice that Paul refers to 'training in righteousness'. To the extent that we are to be involved in one another's 'training', the necessity for on-going involvement is obvious, which, in turn, brings us back to the necessity for stable relationships. The Church, for such a long time, has tried to accomplish both spiritual training, and even reproof, by a simple declaration of the truth. But no skill which requires training is acquired through verbal instruction alone, no matter how clear or well presented the instructions may be. And learning to walk in righteousness requires training indeed! The implication is clear; we must be prepared to get involved with one another and to remain involved while we lovingly assist in one another's training in righteousness. Paul declares, 'And we exhort you, brethren, admonish the idle, encourage the fainthearted, help the weak' (1 Thess. 5: 14).

Let us turn now to those attitudes which are necessary as we assist one another as imperfect, fellow trainees in righteousness. 'Above all things have intense *and* unfailing love for one another, for love covers a multitude of sins – forgives and disregards the offenses of others' (1 Pet. 4: 8, The Amplified Bible). There is simply no way to avoid the fact that we are to love one another first and foremost. Love forms the basis for all other bonds or exchanges within

Christ's Body. If we do not love one another intensely, we won't be able to do anything else of real quality for one another.

But there are several other attitudes which we must also develop in our relationships with one another, if we are to be able to assist each other in mutual restoration where sin is concerned. 'Finally, all of you, have unity of spirit, sympathy, love of the brethren, a tender heart and a humble mind' (1 Pet. 3: 8). Sympathy, or compassion, is an emotion which frightens many of us, particularly where sin is concerned. Somehow, we feel that we cannot remain objective or firm in our convictions if we are too sympathetic. This belief is so strong that every so often one hears a zealous Christian say, 'The one thing I have no sympathy for is . . .' And then follows the name of some behaviour or attitude or ideology. Usually, the person who says such a thing is doing so out of a sense of deep conviction; and, just as often, he expects others to be impressed by his uncompromising stand! But, actually, what he is saying without realising it is, 'The one area in which I am unable to be like Jesus is . . .' There is simply no human error or failing on earth for which Jesus does not have compassion.

Perhaps, at this point, we need to talk about the extremes. We so often use 'spiritual' grounds to justify our lack of compassion. One such scriptural justification is found in Paul's first letter to the Corinthians. The instance deals with a young man who has had improper relations with his stepmother. Paul writes and advises the church to turn him out and to deliver him, as it were, to Satan for reproof. Then, when Paul writes his second letter to the Corinthians, he tells them to restore the young man quickly lest his sorrow be overwhelming. He goes on to say that he had heard that the church body itself was arrogant and would not receive spiritual instruction. In light of that information, he had felt that he needed to know whether or not they would be faithful to hear and carry out the instructions of one who loved them and had brought them into the truth. Apparently, the sin which concerned Paul most was the collective arrogance of the body; and, as soon as he was assured of their faithfulness to receive instruction, he directed them to go immediately and get that young man and to restore him to fellowship. How ironic that such a scriptural account could be used by some to destroy individuals who are in error, or even those who do not conform, and to further the very sort of arrogance which had prompted Paul's writing in the first place.

Again, Paul writes, 'Brethren, if a man is overtaken in any trespass, you who are spiritual should restore him in a spirit of gentleness. Look to yourself, lest you too be tempted' (Gal. 6: 1). The spirit of gentleness, what a necessary ingredient that is! Note that this instruction doesn't sound like the words of one who advocates the expulsion of wayward brethren. As the prophet of old was instructed to speak tenderly to Jerusalem (Isa. 40: 2), so we are told to speak gently to one another, as we love one another back to wholeness and strengthen one another to walk uprightly before the Lord.

Finally, let us look again at Paul's statement in 1 Thessalonians, 'And we exhort you, brethren, admonish the idle, encourage the fainthearted, help the weak, be patient with them all' (1 Thess. 5: 14). Our impatience with one another is well documented. Peter's discussion with Jesus on the subject of forgiving one another is a case in point (Matt. 18: 21–35). It seemed generous to Peter to forgive one who had wronged him seven times, and he tried to get Jesus to affirm his opinion. But Jesus replied that the limit was something more like seventy times seven! Most of us would side with Peter on this issue; in fact, we often say, 'I've said it once and that ought to be enough!' By that, we usually mean that we expect to be heard and understood (and even obeyed) the first time we speak. If only God could expect such responses from us! God forgive our arrogance!

One major barrier which prevents our being compassionate and patient (or even gentle) where sin is concerned is the honest belief that such attitudes would be interpreted as meaning that we actually condone the sin. And, thus, we respond in very cool or stern ways in order to clearly register our disapproval. To correct this misconception, we need to look again at the life of Jesus. He knew so well how to hate sin but love the sinner. He loved sinners both *before* and *after* their conversion. His stand on sin is clearly documented in his teachings and life; his love and compassion are equally well documented in his dealings with all who came to him. Furthermore, he still loves sinners – all of us!

If we look at a listing of the attitudes which we are to have with one another where the sin problem is concerned, it seems familiar indeed: love, sympathy, humility, tenderness, gentleness, and patience. It reads like a restatement of the fruit of the Spirit. In fact, as we discussed in chapter nine, all that we are to one another and all that we do for one another is the work of the Spirit within us. We simply cannot consistently furnish such an array of attitudes from our own resources, but the 'Spirit helps us in our weakness'. Thank God he does, since it is only when these attitudes are available that any one of us can risk an honest revelation or confession to another. As a matter of fact, in each of our relationships, we must make a choice (not always a conscious one) either to build on honesty or deceit; and, unless we have the reassurance which the attitudes we've discussed provide, the only 'safe' choice is deceit.

I would like to emphasise the importance of this dynamic. If you are lacking in the attitudes which we've been discussing, my only option is clear: Since I need your love and acceptance *more* than I need your help and prayers, I am forced to choose acceptance based on deceit rather than risk the rejection which my honesty might bring. Actually, I need both your love and acceptance *and* your help and prayers. And what is more, I really don't want to deceive you; but I must, unless you can assure me that you'll love me no matter what I reveal of myself.

Before leaving our discussion of healing functions within the Body of Christ, I want at least to mention the whole area of gifts, ministries, and callings. The major references to these are found in 1 Corinthians 12, Ephesians 4, and Romans 12. There is no question that many of these 'bodily functions' also provide stability, reassurance, and health for the individual members of the Body of Christ. I am not going to discuss these at length, however, for two reasons. The first is that gifts, ministries, and callings are the functions of the Body which are most often discussed and written about; and, therefore, many fine books and teachings are readily available. The second is that I am most anxious that we begin to appreciate our relationships with one another on a far more basic, less formal level. Individual members of church bodies have offered one another various ministries and talents for hundreds of years, but they have offered themselves so very little and so very seldom. The truth is, we'll be able to receive all manner of ministry from one another far more readily if we are already regularly sharing

144

ourselves with one another. These two levels of sharing should be consistent and simultaneous, 'So, being affectionately desirous of you, we were ready to share with you not only the gospel of God but also our own selves, because you had become very dear to us' (1 Thess. 2: 8).

The only additional point I would like to make about the more formal gifts and ministries is that they, too, follow the principle that we individually possess varied graces in order to be complete in one another:

> Having gifts that differ according to the grace given to us, let us use them: if prophecy, in proportion to our faith; if service, in our serving; he who teaches, in his teaching; he who exhorts, in his exhortation; he who contributes, in liberality; he who gives aid, with zeal; he who does acts of mercy, with cheerfulness (Rom. 12: 6–8).

And, 'As each has received a gift, employ it for one another, as good stewards of God's varied grace' (1 Pet. 4: 10). God help us no longer to despise ourselves or one another because we are not individually complete and self-sufficient. Again, the most natural, healthy state for man is to abide in mutually caring, interdependent, loving relationships.

And now, as we conclude our consideration of loving relationships within the Body of Christ, let us look at some of the ways the Church is being renewed in order that it might provide a framework and encourage a new appreciation for such relationships. The Spirit is increasingly making the Body of Christ a healthier place for people to live and a more effective witness to this our generation. In the final chapter, let us trace some of these newer developments.

12. Renewal Outworked in the Local Body

Renewal is all about change, and personal renewal is all about personal change. Throughout most of our discussion, the changes we have talked about have been those of a rather personal nature, changes which allow us to come together to love and to care for one another better than we have in the past. We've talked about changes in attitudes and behaviour, as well as changes in self-image and ideals. We've also talked about the relevance of these changes to the needs of the current generation, particularly the need for warm, genuine love *and* openness and honesty. But, finally, all of these changes must fit into the larger context of the functioning life of a local body of believers where the members collectively experience loving, shared life and where the world can observe, evaluate, and be drawn into that life. But, here again, change is in order. If the collective life of God's children is ever to become that which God intended, it is absolutely essential that local bodies of believers (whether they call themselves a church, chapel, or fellowship) be prepared for marked changes in both structure and function. If such changes are not allowed, the current renewal will fade as others in the past and with it the hope of both the Church and the world in this our generation. In this final chapter, I would like us to look at some of the newer, more hopeful developments in the Church, particularly those which in some way have begun to provide the necessary setting and encouragement for loving, caring relationships which are so vital to God's promise of full and abundant life.

One of the most encouraging developments is the extent to which the sense of 'family' is developing amongst so many bodies of believers. An outstanding example of a church which has truly become a family is the Church of the Saviour in Washington, DC. The story of this church and the shared life of its members is told in Elizabeth O'Conner's book, *Call to Commitment*. In this church, the sense of family is such that no member is expected to leave the fellowship for such reasons as a better job opportunity elsewhere, or even because of disappointment with the fellowship itself, except as the Lord calls that individual member to another place of service. Furthermore, such a call is expected to be confirmed in the hearts of the whole body. In this particular church body, formal commitment plays a significant role in providing stability and the sense of family. In discussing the extent to which this congregation is a family, Miss O'Conner tells of one member who was recommended for a position in the office of a local business firm where another member of the church was already employed. The second member was refused employment on the basis of the firm's policy to never hire two members of the same family.[1] Even the cold world of business is capable of seeing something spiritual and rather profound when the Church is capable of making it evident.

Another development within the Church which provides for a richer quality of life, most particularly allowing for openness and honesty, is the growing use of small groups. We have already discussed small groups in several contexts, and they are not, historically, a new thing in the Church. The 'class meeting' of twelve believers was an integral part of John Wesley's 'Methodist Society'. The class meeting was, in fact, one of Wesley's 'methods'. More recently, however, there has been a seemingly spontaneous reappearance of small groups throughout the Church. These groups are happening both within the existing church structures and when small numbers of believers from a variety of local churches meet regularly in one another's homes. Such groups are forming on nearly every basis one can imagine, but the thing they all have in common is that such small groups get people closer together than any sort of typical church service or meeting. It is in such closeness that the increased opportunity for openness and honesty is gained.

An example of a church which has made small groups of believers an integral part of their shared life is Old Heritage Wesleyan Church in Scottsdale, Arizona. The story of this church's on-going renewal is told by its pastor, Robert Girard, in the book entitled *Brethren, Hang Loose*. The small groups which have evolved are called 'The Little Churches' to ensure that everyone understands that each group is *in fact* 'the living body of Christ in operation'. One particularly encouraging feature of these 'little churches' is that they each differ from one another. Each group is a composite of the individuals who make it up, and differences from group to group are not frowned upon but understood and appreciated.

In discussing the concerns which led to the forming of the little churches, Girard reports a rather prayerful argument which he had with himself:

> 'Why?' I queried. 'Why is the priestly ministry, the flow of life between cells an exception rather than a general characteristic of church life?'
>
> The answer echoed back from the word pictures of the church in century one: 'Because there is no opportunity in your church for such ministry. You don't really believe in it. And you are, by the very structure of your church, its meetings and its program, keeping such a caring, mutually helpful ministry between members from happening!'[2]

While small groups, in and of themselves, will not guarantee openness and honesty, the opportunity for such encounter is clearly there in ways which it is not in larger numbers and settings. Furthermore, the evidence from throughout the Church would seem to suggest that, given the opportunity and encouragement, people will open their hearts and lives to one another, and the Holy Spirit will work through such openness to empower the Body of Christ to care lovingly for and upbuild itself in love (Eph. 4: 16).

Another development which has great potential is the use of smaller groups within the church as a means of teaching and instruction, as well as fellowship. Trinity Assembly, a rather large Pentecostal church near Los Angeles, is pastored by Don Pickerill. Recently, this church abandoned the traditional American-style Sunday School altogether. Instead, the congregation has been divided into groups of approximately fifty called *chameshems* (the Hebrew word for fifty). The members of these fellowship groups, amongst other things, are helping each other learn how to teach and instruct their children in the knowledge of the Scriptures and Christian principles. The whole approach is based upon the belief that the scriptural pattern calls for fathers and mothers, and the home, to teach children scriptural truths rather than using a church-based 'school' system. The *chameshem* includes the whole family and, as a group, meets each

Sunday to discuss issues and problems, as well as to share in the task of teaching the children. The church has also set one night a week aside for the families in each *chameshem* to visit one another's homes. By such an arrangement, each believer is a member of a small, loving body no matter how large the church as a whole may grow. Large, impersonal churches, like any large impersonal crowd, are such effective hiding places, even for people who deep inside don't really want to hide.[3]

But what about the time that is 'lost' doing such things as: building open, honest relationships; getting together with the 'family'; and having every family involved in training and instructing the children? By and large, the attitude of the Church has been that we have a mission to perform in terms of spreading the Gospel and caring for the needy of this world, and that mission takes priority. While the fact of our commission cannot be denied, the emphasis has often been so 'others' oriented that little or no attention has been paid to the well-being of the members themselves. Somehow, it has been assumed that if Christians were kept busy enough doing 'church work' they would be too busy to think or worry about themselves; and, therefore, they would stay well. We have overwhelming evidence, however, that such is not the case! Problems ignored do not simply heal or go away; they move inside and fester. The only real alternative is to give more time and energy to develop the quality of life amongst believers. Attempts at such solutions, however, often only serve to generate crushing guilt over time 'wasted on ourselves'. The thing we need desperately to see is that Christ's commission to us is to love one another and that he, the Lord, will add the increase: 'And all who believed were together and had all things in common ... And the Lord added to their number day by day those who were being saved' (Acts 2: 44–7). The tragedy is that, when we set out to do evangelism without first creating a family for the new converts to come into, we add those who are saved to some sort of corporation rather than to a living body where all are members one of another.

But let's look now at a few examples in this renewal of evangelism at work through small groups and relationships. In his book, *Open House*, John Tanburn tells of the development and operation of house churches at St Barnabas Cray, Kent. This Anglican church divided the larger parish into

149

nine smaller sub-parishes, each centred in a Christian home. In order to emphasise that these home-based meetings are the gathering of the Body of Christ, they have carefully drawn the distinction between 'home meetings' and 'house church':

A meeting is an event, beginning and ending at particular times; meetings are transitory things, and can be used for a time and then dropped in due course in favour of the next gimmick of evangelistic or parochial techniques. But a church is *people*. It is permanently in existence, even when its members are not assembled; it forms an integral part of the structure and life of the wider church. *A house church holds a home meeting.*[4]

The experiment at St Barnabas Cray, is a real challenge to churches whose life inside the sanctuary is never seen by the world they seek to save. Suburbia can be such a formidable foe to the sharing of the Gospel! But the use of homes as a base for the regular functions of the Body of Christ has very clear and relevant advantages both for the quality of life amongst ourselves and for our witness to the world.[5]

In his discussion of the lessons in evangelism which the Holy Spirit taught them at Old Heritage, Robert Girard says:

Is the purpose of the church, as it comes together, to win the lost? Or do we have our church fellowship confused with our mission in the world?

In the First Century Church, unbelievers became the believers at gatherings of the believers, but that does not seem to be the purpose that brought them together. In Acts 2: 42–47, the Lord added new converts to the church daily, but the reason for gathering together was so that those who were already believers could be taught by the apostles, enjoy spiritual fellowship with one another, remember the Lord's death and its benefits by sharing communion, and pray together.

As they did this, they began to love each other and to care for each other. They became personal enough with each other to notice their brothers and sisters in need. So they started – spontaneously – sharing everything they had together.

And when the doors opened, and they poured into the

150

streets and market places and neighborhoods, the believers were so excited about the way they were loved, the Life they had to share with the world, and about what God was doing for them, in them, among them and through them, that the people they talked to *spontaneously* wanted to get in on the happening.[6]

The final result of the use of such principles as these has meant that Old Heritage has had to divide and form a daughter church in order to accommodate the growth. A richer life amongst believers is still the single most effective tool of evangelism: 'A new commandment I give to you, that you love one another; even as I have loved you, that you also love one another. By this all men will know that you are my disciples, if you have love for one another' (John 13: 34–5).

Another example of evangelism within the renewed Church, one which utilises love and friendship, is the work of the Dilaram Houses headquartered in Heerde, Holland. In this particular case, the evangelism issues from a community style of life rather than the more conventional church pattern, but the commitment to the quality of life is still foremost. They say of themselves, 'But one thing we are committed to is that we are a family first, a community of believers, before we are a ministry. Our function stems from what we are, not vice versa.'[7] True evangelism involves identification and involvement; Jesus was a friend of sinners. These factors form the basis of an approach which Floyd McClung, a leader in the Dilaram ministry, calls 'friendship evangelism'. McClung asks several penetrating questions which search out the very basis of our motives in evangelism:

Do we accept non-Christians? Do we believe we can learn something from them? Do non-Christians know we will listen to their problems without condemning them? Do we accept people as they are? Do we intend to build a friendship whether or not people believe in Jesus or accept what we say about him? Is our love and acceptance of people based on whether or not they will accept what we say, dress as we dress, go to the places we go? If so, our love is conditional. Our friendship is shallow and not really motivated by real love for them as people.[8]

151

Thank God, over and over again, the church in renewal is providing this generation with the Gospel lived out in open, honest lives which offer the world love and friendship, not the Gospel only!

Both within the Church and in the larger society people who are severely bruised and scarred often need the care of those who are trained to give special treatment. I would like to refer again to *Love Therapy* by Paul D. Morris. What a miracle that we live at a time when it is possible, in some quarters, for those who are sick and broken to find not only professional help but love. I recall how encouraged I was a few years ago when so many pastors began to talk about counselling in addition to their preaching ministry. But I recall, too, how soon I discovered that most Christian counselling simply mimicked secular systems of therapy, except that the Christian counsellors were usually less well qualified than their secular counterparts – if we're going to offer technique, we'd better be good at it. But if we're prepared to love truly, we've got something to offer that no technique can provide. Furthermore, love works both ways – the 'counsellor' gets well too!

In speaking of involvement, Dr Morris says:

> Vulnerability is another important part of involvement. It is a wise practice for a therapist of the paracaletic school to share some of his own weaknesses with the patient. He must build the concept with the patient that he [the patient] has something to offer to the therapist's life and experience as well. The idea that 'we are in this thing together, we will bear one another's burdens, and together we will conquer it' is a framework in which involvement is nourished.[9]

This recommendation is a wholly new approach in modern times, for both therapists and clergy. It is, however, the approach which Paul used so effectively (1 Thess. 2: 8).

Finally, I would like to discuss two movements which are peripheral to the more established churches: the house church movement and Christian communities. The house church movement is a rapidly growing body of house fellowships which show many signs of becoming another denomination. I should like to reserve judgment, at this time, as to the wisdom or validity of developing yet another church denomination, however loosely knit or well intended. Even *Church* history has a way of repeating itself! The fact remains, however, that many people are finding a source of love and care in these relatively smaller, less formal gatherings than seems at all possible in the meetings of older, less pliable churches. There seems little doubt that most house churches are offering far more in the way of family and involvement than is true for most church congregations.

Christian communities, also, are appearing in growing numbers, this despite the disappointments which have already befallen communities both historically and in the current renewal. Again, I should like to reserve judgment but point out that communities continue to appeal to many Christians because they offer love, care, family, and a sense of stability all within the framework of the kingdom of God. I must, in all honesty, say that I have found no other style of life so potentially rich and rewarding, and I have the deepest love and affection for those with whom I shared life in community at Post Green. But independent house fellowships and communities need not stand as stark alternatives to the more traditional churches. If established churches will accept renewal and their members begin to offer themselves to one another, church life will certainly move into the homes and the day-to-day life of the members; and we will, again, see community on a broad scale amongst believers. What a sad symptom of a tragic period in Church history that we can find Christian churches which are not communities. If, however, churches refuse, or for any reason fail, to provide loving care and family, we can expect, then, to see a growing number of church members choosing alternative forms of fellowship. In the final analysis, any structure or system deserves preservation only to the extent to which it meets the real needs of its members; the quality of life which is available to the child of God is ultimately the one true measure of the worth of any system or structure within the Body of Christ, since any other measure of 'success' denies God's very intent to provide full and abundant life for his children.

While not every current development within the Church is commendable, by and large, the Church is becoming a much healthier place for human habitation! I find myself grateful again and again that I am alive at such a time in the history

153

of the Church. But, the development of new styles of worship and fellowship within the Church at large, and even within local church bodies, can only provide the means by which loving relationships are encouraged and nourished. For such relationships to be a living reality within the Church, individuals must be prepared to open themselves to one another and to allow the Holy Spirit to teach them how to love. At present, loving relationships of the quality which we've discussed are still in rather short supply, and we've only just begun to see the healing, sustaining potential which can be realised as Christians love one another. But a renewed day is dawning; dare we believe that Christ's prayer for the Church is, again, being fulfilled in our day?

I do not pray for these only, but also for those who believe in me through their word, that they may all be one; even as thou, Father, art in me, and I in thee, that they also may be in us, so that the world may believe that thou hast sent me. The glory which thou hast given me I have given to them, that they may be one even as we are one, I in them and thou in me, that they may become perfectly one (John 17: 20–3).

Epilogue

Had I written this book while Deb and I were still members of the Post Green Community, it would not have included, in all probability, chapters nine, ten, and eleven. Life in the Body of Christ seemed so potentially ideal at that time. When, however, a different leadership structure was introduced into the community, there were those of us who felt that we had to reconsider our continued commitment in terms of the particular calling of the Lord upon our lives and, in due course, left the community. It was then that I had to learn that the Body of Christ was designed to heal the very wounds which can come as a result of our having opened ourselves to one another. Although there are many of us who are no longer officially a part of the community, love and 'family' are not limited to structures or systems. Those of my 'family' who have continued as functioning members of Post Green, as well as those who are no longer there, still have the love and concern of my heart. I pray that the Lord will continue to bless them and continue to work out his purposes for them. Clearly, there is a place in the Church for all manner of fellowships. The fact that any one of us feels that we are not to function in a particular sort of system does not, in and of itself, invalidate such systems as a meaningful part of Christ's Body.

May God help us all to continue to trust him to direct us, individually and collectively, into those places where we can fully function within his Church. May he also help us to go on opening ourselves to one another and not to be fearful of the hurts which come as a result of sharing our imperfect love, in the confidence that through loving relationships in his Body there is provided fullness of life and health and healing that we may be whole.

Notes

1. LET ME BE HONEST

1. For those who would like a brief introduction to various schools of psychological thought, together with a Christian perspective on each subject area, see Harold W. Darling, *Man In His Right Mind* (Paternoster Press, Exeter, 1969).

2. THIS IS MAN

1. Otto Rank, *The Trauma of Birth* (Harcourt, Brace, New York, 1929); *Will Therapy and Truth and Reality* (Knopf, New York, 1945).
2. For a discussion of the development theory of Robert W. White, see Salvatore R. Maddi, *Personality Theories* (Dorsey Press, Homewood, Ill., 1968).
3. Erich Fromm, *The Art of Loving* (Unwin Paperbacks, London, 1957).

3. THE WORLD, THE CHURCH, AND THE JOHN WAYNE SYNDROME

1. George M. Trevelyan, *Illustrated English Social History: 4* (Penguin Books, Harmondsworth, Middlesex, 1964).
2. Samuel Smiles, *Self-Help* (John Murray, London, 1958).
3. *The Definitive Edition of Rudyard Kipling's Verse* (Macmillan and Co., London).
4. Edgar A. Guest, *Collected Verse* (The Reilly and Lee Co., Chicago, 1934).
5. Ibid.
6. See P. Edward Ernest (ed.), *The Family Album of Favourite Poems* (Grosset and Dunlap, New York, 1974).
7. Ibid.
8. J. B. Watson, *Psychological Care of Infant and Child* (Norton, New York, 1928).
9. W. E. Vine, *An Expository Dictionary of New Testament Words* (Marshall, Morgan & Scott, London, 1940).
10. For a very fine and more detailed discussion of the New Testament usage of the Greek terms for love, see Paul D. Morris, *Love Therapy* (Tyndale House, Wheaton, Ill., 1974).
11. For a further discussion of the role of false expectations in modern-day Christianity, see William A. Miller, *Why Do Christians Break Down?* (Coverdale House, London, 1973).

4. THE CULTURE IN REVOLT

1. Erving Goffman, *The Presentation of Self in Everyday Life* (Allen Lane, London, 1969).
2. Eric Berne, *Games People Play* (Penguin Books, Harmondsworth, Middlesex, 1964).
3. Sidney M. Jourard, *The Transparent Self* (Van Nostrand Reinhold, London, 1971).
4. John Lennon and Paul McCartney, 'Eleanor Rigby' (Northern Songs Ltd).

5. Erich Fromm, *Escape From Freedom* (Holt, Rinehart and Winston, New York, 1941). Published in Great Britain under the title: *Fear of Freedom* (Routledge, London, 1942).
6. David Reisman, *The Lonely Crowd* (Yale University Press, New Haven, Conn., 1961).
7. Frieda Fromm-Reichmann, 'Loneliness', *Psychiatry*, Vol. 22, No. 1, Feb. 1959, pp. 1–15.
8. William Schofield, *Psychotherapy: The Purchase of Friendship* (Prentice-Hall, Hemel Hempstead, 1964).
9. James Kavanaugh, *Will You Be My Friend* (Nash Publishing, Los Angeles, 1971).
10. Paul Simons, 'Bridge Over Troubled Water' (Charing Cross Music, Inc.).
11. Harry F. Harlow, 'Love in Infant Monkeys', *Scientific American*, Vol. 200, June 1959, pp. 68–74; Harry F. and Margaret Harlow, 'Learning to Love', *American Scientist*, Vol. 54, No. 3, 1966, pp. 244–72.
12. Rene Spitz, 'Hospitalism', *Psychoanalytic Study of the Child*, Vol. 1, 1945, pp. 53–74.
13. Op. cit.
14. S. Simons and J. Reidy, *The Risk of Loving* (Herder and Herder, New York, 1968).
15. Desmond Morris, *Intimate Behaviour* (Corgi Books, London, 1972).
16. Charles A. Reich, *The Greening of America* (Penguin Books, Harmondsworth, Middlesex, 1972).
17. Alan M. Dahms, *Emotional Intimacy: Overlooked Requirement for Survival* (Pruett Publishing, Boulder, Colo., 1972).
18. Zick Rubin, *Liking and Loving: An Invitation to Social Psychology* (Holt, Rinehart and Winston, New York, 1973).
19. Rosabeth Moss Kanter, *Commitment and Community* (Harvard University Press, Cambridge, Mass., 1972).
20. Herb Goldberg, *The Hazards of Being Male* (Signet Books, New York, 1977).
21. Op. cit.
22. Op. cit.
23. Jeremy Campbell, 'It's the Bond That Makes the Bucks', *Evening Standard*, London, Feb. 2, 1977, p. 17.
24. Ibid.

5. THE CHURCH IN RENEWAL

1. Several fine books have been written on various aspects of the Jesus People movement. An example is Chuck Smith, *The Reproducers* (Regal Books, Glendale, Calif., 1972).
2. Two fine books on the charismatic outpouring in the Roman Catholic church are Kevin and Dorothy Ranaghan, *Catholic Pentecostals* (Paulist Press, New York, 1969); *As The Spirit Leads Us* (Paulist Press, New York, 1971).
3. For a further discussion of the relationship between Church renewal and current social needs, see Michael Griffiths, *Cinderella with Amnesia* (Inter-Varsity Press, London, 1975).
4. John Powell, *Why Am I Afraid to Tell You Who I Am?* (Fontana, London, 1975).
5. William A. Miller, *Why Do Christians Break Down?* (Coverdale House, London, 1973).
6. Gordon Bailey, *Plastic World* (Send The Light Trust, Bromley, Kent, 1971); *Moth-balled Religion* (Send The Light Trust, Bromley, Kent, 1972); *Patchwork Quill* (SOL Publications, Birmingham, 1975).
7. Graham Kendrick, 'My True Feelings' (Thankyou Music).
8. Graham Kendrick, 'Loneliness' (Thankyou Music).
9. Marion Leach Jacobsen, *Crowded Pews and Lonely People* (Tyndale House, Wheaton, Ill., 1975).

10. John Powell, *Why Am I Afraid to Love?* (Fontana, London, 1975).
11. Paul D. Morris, *Love Therapy* (Tyndale House, Wheaton, Ill., 1974).
12. See Robert Webber (ed.), *Rappings* (Tyndale House, Wheaton, Ill., 1971).
13. For a discussion of both the powerful use of small groups and many aspects of man's nature itself, see Cecil Osborne, *The Art of Understanding Yourself* (Zondervan, Grand Rapids, Mich., 1967).
14. Dietrich Bonhoeffer, *Life Together* (SCM Press, London, 1954).
15. Three books which present Christian communities from varied points. of view are Michael Harper, *A New Way of Living* (Hodder and Stoughton, London, 1974); Dave and Neta Jackson, *Living Together in a World Falling Apart* (Creation House, Carol Stream, Ill., 1974); Andrew Lockley, *Christian Communities* (Ave Maria Press, Notre Dame, Ind., 1972).
16. Stephen B. Clark, *Building Christian Communities* (Ave Maria Press, Notre Dame, Ind., 1972).
17. For a fuller discussion of the role of women in the Church, as well as many other current issues of vital importance to Church renewal, see Michael Harper, *Let My People Grow* (Hodder and Stoughton, London, 1977).

6. THE COST OF RENEWAL IS CHANGE

1. See study notes in *New Analytical Bible* (John A. Dickson Publishing Co., Chicago, 1950).

7. LOVING RELATIONSHIPS WITHIN THE BODY OF CHRIST

1. Matthew Henry, *Commentary on the Whole Bible* (Marshall, Morgan & Scott, London).
2. For a further discussion of the renewal of loving relationships within the Body of Christ, see Paul Hinnebusch, *Friendship in the Lord* (Ave Maria Press, Notre Dame, Ind., 1974).

8. THE COST OF LOVING RELATIONSHIPS IS EVEN MORE CHANGE

1. For a more detailed discussion of the need for more personal approaches in psychotherapy and counselling, see William Schofield, *Psychotherapy: The Purchase of Friendship*.
2. By permission of the author, with my loving gratitude.
3. While I would not agree with all that is said by the author about placing intentional limits during later stages of a developing relationship, I would recommend the discussion regarding the legitimate place of rather strong dependency during the earlier, developmental stages of a loving relationship in Paul Hinnebusch, *Friendship in the Lord*.

9. HEALING PROCESSES WITHIN THE BODY

1. Nonsexual, affectionate love is a troublesome concept for many. For additional discussion from another point of view, see ibid.

10. MORE ABOUT HEALING PROCESSES WITHIN THE BODY

1. See Geoffrey Summerfield (ed.), *Voices: The Third Book* (Penguin Books, Harmondsworth, Middlesex, 1968).
2. Antoine de Saint-Exupéry, *The Little Prince* (Pan Books, London, 1974).
3. Graham Kendrick, '*Taking Without Giving*' (Thankyou Music).

4. For a very balanced discussion of the need for Christians to share material possessions, see Max Delespesse, *The Church Community—Leaven and Life-Style* (Ave Maria Press, Notre Dame, Ind., 1973).

11. THE SIN PROBLEM AND THE HEALING PROCESSES

1. For a further discussion of the whole issue of confession, see Cecil Osborne, *The Art of Understanding Yourself.*

12. RENEWAL OUTWORKED IN THE LOCAL BODY

1. Elizabeth O'Conner, *Call to Commitment* (Harper and Row, New York, 1963).
2. Robert C. Girard, *Brethren, Hang Loose* (Zondervan, Grand Rapids, Mich., 1972).
3. Teaching tapes on the role and function of the *chameshem* within local church structure may be obtained from Real to Reel Tape Ministry, 2424 Colorado Blvd., Los Angeles, Calif., 90041, USA.
4. John Tanburn, *Open House* (Falcon Books, London, 1970).
5. For a further discussion of the use of homes as the base for church life, see Ernest Southcott, *The Parish Comes Alive* (Mowbray, Oxford, 1956).
6. Op. cit.
7. Jeff Fountain, 'Is it True What They Say ...?', *Incite*, Vol. 3, No. 1, July 1976, pp. 2–3.
8. Floyd McClung, 'Friendship Evangelism', *Incite*, No. 6, Jan. 1977, pp. 7–9.
9. Op. cit.

Anyone wishing to contact the author may do so at the following address:

The Rev Dr Jim Bigelow
c/o C.D.S.
St Mark's Church Chambers
Kennington Park Rd
London SE11 4PW